ART AND THE DEGRADATION OF AWARENESS

Other Publications by Jeff Nuttall

Verse

The Limbless Virtuoso (with Musgrove)
Songs Sacred and Secular
Poems I Want to Forget
Love Poems
Journals
Poems 1963-68
Penguin Modern Poets No 12 (with Jackson and Wantling)
Objects
Sun Barbs
Grape Notes/Apple Music
Scenes and Dubs
Mad witth Music
Twenty-Two Poems

Fiction

Mr Watkins Got Drunk and Had to be Carried Home
The Case of Isabel
Pig
The House Party
The Gold Hole
Snipe's Spinster
Anatomy of my Father's Corpse
What Happened to Jackson
Muscle
The Patriarchs

Non Fiction

Man / Not Man
Bomb Culture
Common Factors / Vulgar Factions
King Twist, A Portrait of Frank Randle
Performance Art Vol. I: Memoirs
Performance Art Vol. II: Scripts
The Pleasures of Necessity

ART AND THE
DEGRADATION
OF AWARENESS

JEFF NUTTALL

CALDER PUBLICATIONS
LONDON

RIVERRUN PRESS
NEW JERSEY

First Published in Great Britain in 2001 and in the USA in 2001 by Calder Publications Ltd and by Riverrun Press.

ISBN 0 7145 4293 8

British Library cataloguing in Publications Data.
A catalogue record of this title is available from the Library of Congress.

Library of Congress cataloguing in Publication Data.
A catalogue record of this title is available from the Library of Congress.

Typeset printed by Newton Design & Print Ltd, London, UK
www.newtondp.co.uk

CONTENTS

INTRODUCTION

The last year of every century is indicated by two noughts – double nothing, two blind blanks, two pickled eggs, a blocked shotgun muzzle. When they crop up at the end of a millenium the opportunity is there for a bigger than usual eczema of fin-de-siecle alchemy and clairvoyance. When they cropped up in the middle of Tony Blair's first term of office they glowed on his screen as the perfect logo for his policy, an emptiness which seeks to sidestep and jettison its impediments – such things as memory, membership, loyalty, tradition, empirical truth, ethics and politics. The guns to which people had stuck had to be dismantled and left to rust in the Twentieth Century. Shortly after his election Blair announced that, in his opinion, ideology had had its day. With these two luminous noughts he could impose his curfew. The new could only be achieved if the old could be declared to have been terminated.

Blair seemed astute in appeasing something that had been making itself evident in society for at least forty years, an impatience with the past, that mind-movie of tedious old men with their relish for difficulty. Brian Thompson came across it while holidaying on the English south coast four years ago, sitting at a pavement café next to a cockney family, father, mother and teenage son, with the town war memorial across the road.

'Wassat then?' asks the son. 'That stone thing?'

'Do you really not know?' asks Brian.

'Would I ask?'

'What does it say?'

'For the fallen.'

'Well?'

'Suddink to do with racing?'

Brian, who is a deep admirer of the poetry of the '14 – '18 war poets, proceeds to tell the boy about the trenches, the Somme, Paschendael etc.

'Ere,' intercedes the father. 'We don't wanna know about no fuckin' wars. We're on 'oliday. We don't want tellin' about no fuckin' wars.'

Norman Rosenthal, director of the Royal Academy on Piccadilly, sensed that Blair had found this particular pulse when he approached Cabinet ministers for someone to open the Monet exhibition. There was much difficulty until Gordon Brown, after having been asked twice, agreed to open the show.

'What was the problem?' asks Rosenthal.

'We've been told not to be photographed next to anything old,' replied the Chancellor.

After all, a mosque in which the public was to be addressed, both visually and verbally, in a manner suitable for lower junior schools, as though people had been rendered infantile by mandatory amnesia, was already under construction at Greenwich. In the event the sight of the anxious Blair, shakily maintaining his identificatory grin alongside a stonily unamused Queen, certainly told the story of the agony and stress it takes to mount such ostentatious vacuity.

As though to buoy up this luckless squib it was declared that Millennial Celebration was to be a continuum in the year of the great Double Zero. All events of that year were to be understood as a procession of Millennial Spectacles. Our crazy clothes were to be millennial. Our computed tunes were to be millennial. Maybe even our wars and 'flu epidemics and rail crashes were to be understood as positive elements in our new beginning. Double Blind was to mean unique. History having been forgotten, anything millennial would be a first. The new beginning was a truly millennial new beginning because we didn't have to begin it. We just had to block out memory. We weren't cleaning the slate in order to do more sums. Millennially speaking it was vital that we lose the slate. The stupid were at last admitted to their kingdom, plain for all to see on breakfast television and in journalism reduced to mob slogans. Decisions were to be confined to freely gestating electro-technology. Who needs a brain when we have the Internet?

With ideology obsolete all the Cabinet need do is drink de-caf and swap holiday snaps. The spinners, those dedicated cultivators of stupidity, will issue their instructions at all levels. The consensus is compulsory and if any Ken Livingstone shows maverick tendencies, well, democracy must not stand in our way in preventing this damaging return to politics.

But even now it can be seen that amnesia does not come so readily to the human brain, however culturally disabled it may be. Livingstone was elected in defiance of assumed consensus and not enough people want to go to the adventure playground at Greenwich. Perhaps one or two of us recall from the previous century that, among the blood baths and pathetic political disasters there was ideology enough to correct its own fractures and art enough available for public use with sufficient vitalising excellence to reignite humanity's short-lived dream of determining its own destiny. Such aspirations must be dealt with by subtler strategies than monster circus tents. Worship held people in captivity and it is still useful. Put the art in a building as awesome as a cathedral. Spiritualise this raw nourishment of the public psyche and the public have once more been redefined as passive consumers, not as inspired participants. In the Tate Modern, art, like ideology, can be consigned to its spectacular tomb.

This book was written, re-written, altered, edited and written yet again during the last years of the Twentieth Century. It is pre-millennial, an important keepsake.

Its first draft was a pamphlet called Marketing Revolt, a rant based, more or less, on my perceptions of changes in social and professional surroundings and my attempt to understand them. Since then I have noted each time anyone proudly touts as policy that which I originally feared as decay.

The Millennial Double Zero vindicated all my fears. In the glare of malfunctioning fireworks it substantiated and illuminated one man's experience of this unique fusion of degradation, political hubris and infantile greed.

My thanks are due to Chris Hall, my son Toby, the late Tom Northey, Ann Wolff, Jeff Rees and Robert Bank for providing me with much useful discussion. Robert Bank's help with research was greatly valued. My brother A.D. Nuttall and Professor Tim Jones were good enough to read the earlier manuscript and make useful corrections. John Calder, as always, has been a most rigorous editor. Thanks are also due to Barbara Heatherington and Caenwen Jones for long hours at the keyboard. Philippa Beale gave me two opportunities to read lengthy sections to her students and Wolverhampton University invited me to give a reading which Andrew Calcutt transcribed for the sadly defunct LM Magazine.

We are a young species but we are too old for new starts. Repair the quadrant and resume the original voyage.

PART ONE

INITIAL INFORMATION

In my craft and sullen art
Exercised in the still night
When only the moon rages
And the lovers lie abed
With all their griefs in their arms,
I labour by singing light
Not for ambition or bread
But for the common wages
Of their most secret heart.

Not for the proud man apart
From the raging moon I write
On these spindrift pages
But for the lovers, their arms
Round the griefs of the ages
Who pay no praise or wages
Nor heed my craft or art.

Dylan Thomas

1.   DUMBING DOWN

Liverpool, 1981.
The Albert Dock is clear in pale golden blocks of late afternoon light through the vast window that forms one wall of the Granada Liverpool studio. The audience and main speakers are banked adjacent to it and the rectangles of sunlit warehouses are reflected in the spectacles of Waldemar Janusczak, the well-known art critic. Opinions roll concerning the quality, the need for, the importance of, the possibility of, art on Merseyside. I am there with a group from the Art School where I am head of Fine Art.

We consider a bad depictive painting, realistic, skilled and insensitive. We consider a painting in the non-figurative manner of the late '50s, early '60s, held up for us by the artist, a pleasant middle-aged woman who completed a course at Liverpool Art School some years previously. It's interesting to note that Stuart Sutcliffe's painting in the collection of the Walker Gallery is a fine strong work in the mode, reflecting the strong teaching of Arthur Ballard, then an able and powerful non-figurative painter. Sutcliffe's gestures of paint are posed within the four straight lines defining the edge of the canvas. His colours are muted, reacting one against the other with a subtle optical resonance. This woman's painting is mediocre, in no particular way different from millions of works pouring out of British art schools in those optimistic years of St Ives and Basic Design. The forms are exuberant but arbitrary. There are too many colours and the colours are not sufficiently controlled for them to set up any unity, one against the other, within the work's boundaries. And the surface is careless and slack. Art schools now, in the mid-Eighties, have withdrawn from the rigour of critical conviction that Harry Thubron tried to develop into a visual system that would equal the musical harmonic systems of tonic solfa in the Fifties and Sixties. Pop Art, Conceptual Art, the scepticism of the Structuralists towards individual vision, the hostility of the feminists towards the assured gestural impulse, have all served to dismantle the coherence of art education. Even Arthur Ballard has stopped painting after reading Tom Wolfe's essay The Painted Word. Increasingly we are reduced to debate and increasingly debate is dominated by the glib litanies of Political Correctness.

Finally we are asked by the Granada production team to consider the work of a free improvising jazz group amongst whom I recognise Terry Day. I recall Terry's work with the early People Show, his dedication, his instant ability to relate his paradiddles and his volcanic rim-shots to actions in space and dialogue, and his spacy understanding of the absurd. The group are professional artists of some skill and long-standing. They interweave each other's patterns with familiarity, understanding and dynamic grace. Most of them have survived the Sixties interfusion between Alexis Korner's Rhythm and Blues movement and the diatonic holocausts of free jazz. What they play here is music with a delicate texture, informed by extending a respectful ear to percussive musical systems in Africa and the East. They are also funny, deporting themselves with knowing eccentricity, gnostic goonery.

Januszczak, when asked which of these pieces he thinks of merit, says he isn't able to tell and he doesn't think anyone else is either. True value, he says like the good Courtauld scholar that he is, can only be assessed at the distance of a century or two. He suspects that everything here will be seen to be worthless. Later, in the Nineties, he will become a commissioning editor for Channel Four and use his position to present a programme attempting to dismiss Twentieth Century art on the grounds of its unproclaimed Blavatskyism. He will follow this in '98 with the truly absurd The Truth about Art in which his total bankruptcy in areas of aesthetic perception will lubricate a kind of teeny-bopper trivialisation of creative brilliance. Simultaneously he will become Charles Saatchi's adviser on what to buy next.

I ask him if he cannot hear that the band knows what it's doing, in placing notes with great instrumental skill to express and engender considerable excitement, that the paintings are not composed with such certainty of professional purpose, nor success of professional skill. The players have their notes in exactly the right places. The painters have their marks and their colours in roughly the right places. Is he not aware of this?

'Are you claiming ?' he begins, with that dry scepticism so frequently heard when the scholarly talk about the pleasures of art. I am shocked to hear it. Why is he drawn to art if his pleasure ducts are dead to it? He is without the information that his profession requires and he is not open to sensitisation.

'Shall we move on?' says the presenter, slightly embarrassed.

Imagine a surgeon turning round to the waiter in his club and saying 'Look, I'm enjoying this meal and I don't want to cut it short. Here's a scalpel. Go and carry out a brain operation for me. Tell 'em I said it was okay.' If this occurred there would be consternation because the waiter wouldn't do. When it comes to surgery we still respect, need and demand specialist knowledge. In the matter of cutting up our bodies we don't risk ambiguities. We assume that there are certainties in the field of the surgeon and we put faith in the disciplines that teach them. Cancer is a pretty unequivocal fact. We know it results in death unless treated. We trust the qualified surgeon to carry out the treatment. The discipline and the faith in the discipline hold firm.

If, however, a painter told the waiter to finish his painting, or the poet told the waiter to knock out a couple of poems for his next slim volume, or the saxophonist told the waiter to go and do his set at Ronnie Scott's, there would be no deep concern. Nor would anybody object too much if a philosopher sent the waiter to take his seminar, if a scientist sent the waiter to check his statistics or if a politician sent the waiter to sit in Parliament for an hour or so. Certainly a few isolated figures would be displeased, but there would be widespread indifference among the general public. What is more worrying is that there would be no firm action of censure within the professional areas of art, philosophy, science and politics. Tenuously we retain a faith in our present point

13

of progress in surgery. Weirdly we have abandoned any notion of desirable progress in our ethics and aesthetics. Improvement of the civilisation by high-level mental ability or manual skill carries little clout at the close of the Twentieth Century.

This is not totally true of course. We love entertainment and art will continue to be a matter of concern when it takes place within the scope of entertainment. We love fashion, and art will be acknowledged when it contributes to fashion. Similarly science will command supportive interest when it contributes to technology. Politics will attract an audience if it promises more money. Philosophy will command respect when it grants pre-eminence to entertainment, technology and wealth.

Beyond this a vengeful disdain is in operation. It has been some time since cubism, serial composition, stream of consciousness, quantum mechanics, economic theory, and existentialism put painting, music, literature, science, politics and philosophy outside the scope of public comprehension. In the midst of this bewilderment the public have suspected charlatans, resented the wealth, power and esteem of many practitioners, and have resented that so much is being done to them and for them which they didn't invite and which they don't see the point of.

They had to suffer this estrangement because the intellectuals of the Nineteenth Century demanded and got a clear run. The only way to impede them was by argument and nobody could argue with the best brains. Civilisation was forced upon the mass either in the guise of good taste, hygiene, Bauhaus architecture, Nazi-ism, Communism, education or law, by individuals who demanded a bland and limitless trust.

They demanded this trust because they believed themselves to be informed. Secretly in the ecumenical middle-ages, defiantly since the Renaissance and messianically since the Enlightenment, intellectuals had been in pursuit of truth by exploration and experiment, urgently and daringly transgressing the closed and static paradigms of religion and consensus.

Pursuit of truth often went in two stages, through the postulation (the earth is global and we can travel its circumference) and demonstration (I have made the trip and finished up at my starting point.) The theory (the postulation) was metaphysical. The proof (the demonstration) was empirical. Other theories in various intellectual fields were: imaginary narratives enhance an awareness of the world; the premise that matter is composed of minute magnetic fragments; humanity exists independently of divine intervention; the statement that nature evolves from species to species; human individuals can and should decide their own actions; space, colour, form, sound and surface may generate positive and valuable human response outside codes of meaning so that the Christian may be uplifted by a mosque and Muslims by the cathedral.

Many of the truths at the theoretical stage were shown to be untrue at the demonstration stage — the phlogiston theory, for example. Many remain unconvincingly or incompletely demonstrated, Freud's Oedipus complex for instance. The assumption among the intellectuals was, however, that the more we ascertained what was true about humanity's surroundings and humanity's well-being, humanity's capability, its past and its future, the more we could divert the continuum of our existence from that of a predecided destiny (God's will) to a process of self-generated development (evolution). Then we could take our place in programmes of self-directed improvement (history and progress). One area in which the demonstration of the sought-after truth was impressively successful was in engineering technology. The carriage actually did move without the horse. The glass bulb gleamed without flame. The aeroplane left the ground. The benefits were immediate and wildly seductive. The credibility then afforded to the technologist prolonged the credibility, or at least the tolerance, extended to the philosopher, the psychologist, the mesmerist, the artist and the revolutionary politician. The empirical evidence that the darkness vanished when the house was wired and the switch clicked and that the carriage moved when the fuel was ignited, did not encompass any real comprehension of what electricity exactly was, or what those little popping explosions might eventually do to your lungs.

Most people belonged to a labouring, exploited working class. Many of the intellectuals declared themselves to be champions of the working class, promising various ways of relieving them of exploitation, poverty and ignorance. Money, of which the mass had insufficient, was the enemy, the root of all evil. The way to overpower money was to learn and to work for the common good, to participate in the debate and the organisation of the system, to throw one's faith in the illimitable future of humanity freed from money which seemed, for the mass, to spell slavery.

By the late Twentieth Century the masses had discovered that they didn't want progress except insofar as it served their simple desires for luxury, leisure and status. The fate of humanity was no single person's concern any more than human aspirations to self-determination or greater justice were any single person's concern. Preaching intellectuals were a drag and a pretentious drag at that, when the simple desires of the mass met far greater respect among the entrepreneurs of a new and vastly better equipped popular culture. McDonalds, Colonel Sanders, Levis, Walt Disney, Elvis Presley and Internet didn't demand any unusual intelligence and sported no mystification. Furthermore wealth had transmuted from the exploitation of the mass by labour to the exploitation of the mass by appeasement of their simplest tastes.

Nobody was telling anybody in the new popular culture that they were making fools of themselves by their fondness for Mickey Mouse. Here was sanction for their low understanding and prestige in their possession of the latest product. A pair of trainers was worth more in terms of status than a degree or a skill.

The computerised international consumer manufacturer had, even by the '80s, visibly outflanked those old tyrants the government and the law. The dealer made no more demands on you than your money. There was no need to work for distinction when you could buy it.

Those previously privileged specialists in the advancement of civilisation had been left high and dry. So many of the theories had failed. The theories that Marx and Engels formed in France and London failed in demonstration in Russia and Eastern Europe. The theory that self-determination would lead to happiness and leisure had failed in demonstration when it led to perpetual struggle and a wrestling with reason that increasingly had to be entrusted to the egghead who had got us in this fix in the first place. Fair distribution proved to be mere self-denial. Party membership proved to be another face of exploitation.

What if they were in possession of the truth, those eggheads? If so many truths failed in application who wanted truth? What was it anyway? If you were interested in it, one would do as well as another. A certain degree of vengeful delight was evident when these fields of speciality were thrown open to the figurative waiter, that is, to the untrained, the inept, the stupid and exploitative. Great prizes were awarded for fabrications presented as art which were not art. Philosophy departments in universities were starved, decimated and closed. In the newly thriving areas of cultural studies, media studies, market studies and women's studies, philosophy was held up to triumphant ridicule licensed by new analyses that cast the possibility of progress into doubt and certainly removed the task of improvement from the shoulders of the individual.

Critics, so trained through the offices and studios of the media, lubricated the dissolution of critical and ethical values as fast as they could. Virtual reality exhibitions thrived as hospitals closed. Serial killers became role models as the Third World reverted to tribal barbarity.

The masses remained stodgily indifferent, plastic baseball cap reversed, Coke can in hand, or crowed triumphantly when the mediocrity for which their parents and grandparents had been made to cringe frisked blithely in a market where good and bad, true and untrue, the creative and the destructive, the beautiful and the ugly, the brilliant and the pathetic, were all equally available at a floating value and where nothing would ever again be held to be anybody's fault.

True and false were, by now, universally held to be a matter of opinion. Humanity inhabited a forum of notions which were equal in weight and relative. Because human rights were equal, then the variability of perceptions of truth from culture to culture must also be held to be equal. It was only when it came to surgery that some people were conceded to be closer to the truth than others. There being no certain truth or untruth it was easy to declare morality relative. The roots of morality in empathy and affect were lost to view. The root of empathy and affect in spontaneous biological family instinct was decried.

Debates of current issues were carried on by radio and television with less and less emphasis on informed opinion and ever greater emphasis on the opinions of the masses who, brought into their own at last, could belligerently spout their own lame bigotries in the faces of celebrity linkmen whose key to the debate was increasingly their willingness to tolerate and 'dumbdown' to the level of the mass. Michael

Parkinson, David Frost, Jeremy Paxman and Jimmy Young opened up the field in the Sixties, Seventies and Eighties – two journalists, a comedian whose satirical material was somehow allowed to give him political credibility, and an ageing dance-band singer become disc-jockey. Politicians were happy to occupy the sofa alongside starlets and somnoloquent rock singers in order to attain the guaranteed media audience of millions.

Oprah Winfrey changed all that in the late Eighties. A pugnacious buck-friendly honours graduate in the University of Life, she had the down-home, I've-been-there-too approach tempered with the modulated condemnatory ring of the gospel preacher. Discussion descended here to the level of the chapel ceremony called Giving Testament. An endless procession of victims raked their memories for trauma as they made the lounge-lozenge by contributing to the perpetual litanies of child abuse, rape, harassment, bulimia, anorexia, tobacco-abuse, alcoholism, transsexuality — virtually anything to obviate any discussion of politics, science, technology or culture. Her approach to truth was fuelled by such a pitch of barely contained hysteria that the verification of accusation and the testing of wild recollection was impossible. Esther Rantzen, who had previously presented a comedy programme, doglegged into this new confessional tradition. Other presenters brought the mode into the pornographic field by extending the confessional field to orgasm, underwear and bodily proportions. The confessional platform was a great place to say what the hell you liked and be taken seriously provided you'd suffered enough.

And here, as though facilitated by the change in the mode of the debate brought about by such programmes, were politicians like Thatcher and Blair who were prepared to change any beliefs and principles that obstructed their election. They stood on platforms only recently occupied by Enoch Powell and Aneurin Bevan. Socialism and patriotism were both scrapped for a pragmatic sparring with the psychopathic market. In the new world of floating values nobody stopped them. Most people applauded.

Here came the Structuralist thinkers like Derrida, Lacan, Althusser, and Post-Modernists like Baudrillard and Lyotard, occupying the places recently vacated by Wittgenstein, Sartre and Heidegger. They were intellectuals who fed the common distrust of intellectuals with their varyingly successful pursuit of the truth by totally altering the understanding of the truth. Freudian therapists had long been allowing their patients a variety of individual truths ('I believe it's true for you.') Now Structuralists were following a line of thinking that led from Vico through Wittgenstein, Levi-Strauss, Saussure and Chomsky. Truth, they contended, was algebraic, so, if a contention took its place as a working element in the society's equation of belief, it was true. Truth which resulted from the observation of reality was different, they said, and was anyway impossible. People did not make societies. Societies made people, each one of whom was unable to see beyond the range of experience belonging to the society. This cancelled the democracy of individual truths afforded by Freudian therapy but insisted on a democracy of truths from culture to culture, with Buddhism equal to Islam, Mohammed to Christ, Christ to Marx, Marx to Henry Ford. If the whole span of possible truth was culturally determined and the culture enjoyed a sovereignty previous to, and totally governing, human decisions, then truths were comparative, variable and determined by collective belief. They could even be called fictions – *'verum factum, verum fictum.'* In terms of the stains left by their own prematurely abandoned Marxism, science and philosophy were anyway dismissable as bourgeois ideology and its shadow, Stalinist ideology. To replace ideology with a better ideology was to continue in a discredited practice. Negation (deconstruction) was the only possible position to take said Derrida. Post-modernists Lyotard, Deleuze and Guattari advocated 'incredulity to meta-narratives' by which they meant science, metaphysics and aesthetics. In Baudrillard's 'hyper-reality' real things had been replaced by their fictitious images in the media. This had certainly occurred in the brains of TV-hypnotized people but Baudrillard declared, with all seriousness, that the Gulf War had not really happened, words that doubtlessly comforted Tony Blair and Bill Clinton when they 'degraded' (*sic*) Iraq for the second time.

If truth and its pursuit by courageous and brilliant individuals was devalued by Structuralism, quality was devalued by Post-Modernism. The genius, the virtuoso and the master craftsman were only the result of the culture that pursued the mythology in which they were granted a role. They had no more claim to validity or credibility than the cack-handed, the charlatan or those afflicted as the pathetic Branwell Brontë had been afflicted, by nave hubris. Hype was as good as talent and talent was really only a notion, a fading residue from artisan culture. Increasingly the pronouncements of such kamikaze intellectuals rephrased contentions that were put with greater rhetorical wit in the journalism of Tom Wolfe, in the media performances of Desmond Morris and Marshall McLuhan. Irony replaced vision as the guiding mode of the work, but this was a slight irony, not to be compared with Swift or Nathaniel West.

Self-styled Post-Modern artists arrived – Damien Hirst, Rachel Whiteread and Mark Wallinger who replaced Francis Bacon, John Bellany, Philip King, Henry Moore. Their theft of the 'art' syllable and their re-application of it to advertising imagery confirmed that art, too, addressed itself to deconstruction and freed itself of any pathetic delusions by which history had been benighted.

Critics like Tim Hilton and Waldemar Januszcak replaced Kenneth Clarke, John Berger, Patrick Heron, Bronowski and Wilenski, and wrote about the achievements of the new artists, seemingly unable to see with any certainty that achievements had been studiously avoided. And here came the poets John Hegley, Craig Raine, Murray Lachlan-Young and Fiona Pitt-Keighley, enjoying the importance once allotted to Dylan Thomas and W. H. Auden, masking the achievements of the completely unacknowledged poetry renaissance in the United Kingdom, Bill Griffiths and Maggie O'Sullivan remaining almost unknown, and poetry cleared from the shelves of the bookshop in the Institute of Contemporary Arts.

In every field, merit was no longer measured in terms of insight, skill, innovation, beauty or honour. The yardstick was popularity which meant saleability which meant price. Any nuance of the old egghead world of certainty through outstanding intelligence and sensitivity, was not only no longer necessary; it had to be rigorously avoided by anyone seeking fame and fortune.

Values had never before been so clear and simple as to be numerically ordered by the consensus of the market. The paying game was the American one that anybody can play. Winners played it. Dissidents lost. In such a society they had anyway been declared redundant. In all areas but those governed by genetic imperatives of self-preservation, the waiter, as I have described him, was welcome. Post-Modernists would have even given him the scalpel.

2. THE ART FACT

> – not for the glory and least of all for the profit, but
> to create out of the human spirit something which
> did not exist before.
>
> William Faulkner

Leeds, 1967.
Jim Haynes looks pleased to see me despite his fatigue. Those button eyes brighten a little and a hand descends on my shoulder. I know that the only sleep he's been able to grab has been on the train from King's Cross. It's '67 and his Arts Laboratory has succeeded beyond his wildest expectancies as he opened door after door to new possibilities. The original devotion to difficult and challenging art which had shaped the ambience at the Edinburgh Traverse has changed into a self-determined process of interaction between the hordes of the alienated young crowding his Drury Lane premises looking for drugs, unimpeded sex and a transformed culture of music and style. Jim, as the tolerant and openly lecherous father of this new vast tribe, is busy every night, all night, particularly because his spaces, designed as galleries, theatres and bookshops, have been subtly colonised as crash pads. The cinema is a nightly, night long, group-grope. Only a week or two ago, a young man walked onto the middle of the stage area during a People Show, unrolled his sleeping bag and turned in. Police are never far away, looking for runaways and drugs. Haynes has taken on this difficult pastoral role because he believes that he had certain duties to perform at a fulcrum of cultural transformation that will, first, save the world, and then reorganise it around the positive human attributes of love, generosity, tolerance and joy. He is here at Leeds University to talk about this. I am at Leeds to talk about art, what it is, what it does, what it must do in the current political dilemma.

19

Our talk takes place in a vast hall. We take chairs and ask our audience to re-arrange their rows of chairs in a semi circle around us.

I notice two old buddies in the audience who are to be instrumental in getting me a job at the art school down the road. They are Olly Accola from Norwich, a keen supporter and follower of the Australian Dancers, and Robin Page who used to work at the Dover Street ICA, a hangdog man with a ragged beard and crazy responsive eyes.

Halfway through my account of the artist's experience a thick-set student with myopic spectacles and curly hair suddenly leans forward in his seat and then, straightaway, taking advantage of the moment's silence this had achieved, he asks 'What's your authority for all this?'

'I'm an artist,' I say. 'I'm describing what I do.'

'By what right are you an artist?'

This is my first encounter with those who, rather than study a practice, study other people who have already studied the practice. I am later to meet them in great numbers – those who don't climb the mountain but compare interpretations of the accounts of those who did.

Perfect pitch is not an uncommon human gift. People who have perfect pitch are able to identify, out of silence, the true notes of the scale. They carry true pitch with them and they immediately know whether or not a single instrument or a whole orchestra is sharp or flat of the true pitch.

The notes they hold to be true do not vary from individual to individual. All persons with perfect pitch maintain the same middle C. Nor is their ability the result of training, culture or conditioning. It is more in the nature of the rapid mathematical ability some people are blessed or cursed with. It is not a phenomenon exclusive to the Tonic Solfa system. Indians and Chinese with perfect pitch can equally well pitch the glissandos and quarter-tones of their systems to the true.

Perfect pitch is a phenomenon, an aurally perceptible mathematical constant, a fact and not a notion.

Normally orchestras are not too impeded by it. If a piano is flat it is quite usual for the entire unit to tune to the piano. But if any instrument is out of tune with the agreed pitch there is no doubt about the fault in its pitch by comparison with the other instruments in the unit who will correct the errant instrumentalist. Members of the orchestra, or the audience, who were unaware of the faulty instrument's pitch, are not so aware in their appraisal of the situation as those who were aware and demanded its correction.

As there are people with perfect pitch, so there are people who are tone deaf. The aimless notes and non-notes of tone-deaf people when they sing or play is painful for people with accurate ears. It's no use for the tone deaf to proclaim that their sounds are democratically as good as anyone else's. Their notes are not the notes intended and this is a fact. The ability to perceive the truth is as unfairly distributed as any other ability. Nonetheless, however politically unfair it may be, the orchestra must correct the out-of-tune musician because his divergence is not an alternative but a factual error. He stumbles in the same dark as the waiter probing at a brain tumour with a scalpel. He is not only different. He is wrong.

People who expel the waiter from the operating theatre may well leap to the defence of the out-of-tune musician. The world has been unfriendly to facts since it became clear to the mass that eggheads were far from infallible and that there were an awful lot of facts to be assimilated if anyone was to check up on the eggheads. Putting beauty in the eye of the beholder was perhaps the first attempt to dismantle the fact and demote it to the realm of ambiguity and opinion. This reaction gained considerable credibility when philosophy, instead of voicing new visions like Nietzche's or new scepticisms like Voltaire's, began to devote its time to the analysis of the lexicon rather than the coining of the word. The philosophical question changed from 'What do we see?' to 'How do we see?' Linguistics superseded metaphysics. The extraordinary belief that we can think no more than we have words for replaced the obvious fact that we coin words constantly to serve new thoughts. Our syntax changes similarly, in order to articulate new rhythms of thought and new patterns of communicative relationships.

Originating in Wittgenstein and Saussure this belief was a major root of Semiology, Structuralism and Post-Modernism in France and Britain. Thought and perception served language. Human appraisal of reality was completely determined by the culture which changed according to some tacit consensual process of its own, impervious to dissent, correction or redirection by individuals which the lamentable Althusser proclaimed non-existent. It's chilling now to recognise Althusser's 'The subject does not exist' as the philosophical catalyst to Thatcher's 'Society does not exist.' Although one may seem to be anti-individual and the other exclusively individualist both deny any potency to the altruistic individual.

In this drift towards the devaluing of human thought, truth, the way it had been understood and pursued by Plato, Aristotle, Spinoza, Galileo, Kant and Hegel, and is still understood by surgeons, engineers, police detectives and law courts, was abandoned. In its place we now have an irrelevant possibility hovering forever outside the range of human versions of the truth, a field of blandly relative mythologies in which the fundamentalism of Islam became equal to the European respect for free expression. Society, by some kind of tacit concern for physical safety, retained credibility for the specialists who repaired aeroplanes, cars, hearts, limbs and kidneys. But when the ambience created by the ambivalence of truth spread to aesthetics and ethics, the artist, by whom I mean the creative writers, musicians, painters and sculptors, turned away in a private and mutual abstention from the new direction. Much as women in early Freudian lectures on penis-envy and vaginal orgasm walked quietly out of the lecture theatre, so the artists stepped back from the debate because they knew by their keener senses what the musicians of true pitch knew. This was a discourse of minds that had no experience of unequivocal fact. The aesthetic mandates, imperatives and certainties that continually necessitate creative work in aesthetics may not be as verifiable as true pitch is verifiable by a tuning fork, but it is just as certain, a fact to be sought and struck, not a notion to be launched. All artists know that good and bad in the arts is a matter of proximity to the fact or distance from it. Art works according to natural principles. It is a matter of distress, alienation and bitterness to many artists that so few people know whether they are in tune or not. Aesthetic excitement, which is the way in which successful art registers itself, is close to sexual excitement. Some thinkers, Anton Ehrenzweig for example, have claimed that aesthetics are the sublimation of frustrated sexual excitement.

Unhappily there is no ambiguity about the success or failure of lovemaking. Whoever the lover ought to find exciting according to social codes, or whoever the lover wants to find exciting according to moral codes, the vital element of excitement is fugitive, emerging unbidden and remaining impervious to the will. In the male its presence is clearly visible in an erection. Its absence is clearly revealed in a limp penis.

Aesthetic excitement is equally elusive although no part of the body so clearly registers its presence. As an expert lover can contrive the combination of mental and physical stimulii to provoke an erection, so can an artist put materials together, sounds together, words together, to provoke aesthetic excitement. The excitement may be delightful or it may be distressing as the orgasms of the raped. Whichever, it is deliberately contrived and, artists believe, humanly beneficial.

Whenever civilisation encounters the material with which it must work, the received conditions of nature, it runs into difficulties arising from nature's amorality. This is particularly true in the practice of art. The ability to enjoy the aesthetic is like the ability to enjoy sexual excitement insofar as it is a matter of sensitivity. A lover knows that it is difficult to excite a person of low or damaged libido however much that person may be entitled to a sex life. An artist knows that it is difficult to excite a public whose ears and eyes are dull. He also knows that beyond the dulling and sharpening of senses which cultural conditioning may impose, there is a biological reality to be grasped. However strong may be a citizen's claim to a fair enjoyment of art, some sad souls will never hear or see authentic achievement and these souls are found at all levels of society. By the same token some individuals will leap to a precocious appreciation which cuts across any assessment of their cultural rights. Because art has this power to communicate on a fortuitous biological basis, outside the control of any social consensus, it is periodically marginalised. An aware artist understands this marginalisation because he recognises it as the price he must pay for the power of subversion he inherits in the pre-social area of aesthetics and for his access to that truth, which, in Marcuse's words, 'happens in the estranging language,' with 'images which make perceptible, visible, and audible that which is no longer, or not yet, perceived, said, and heard in everyday life.' He has not yet completely understood that the society which is developing around him at the start of the Twenty First Century not only finds him undesirable. It goes further. He is proclaimed to be impossible. He is an individual who has devoted himself to the experience which is available to his individual awareness, to flavours, qualities, energies and, even more, to objective information which is uniquely available to him and which it is his isolated duty to provide for others. The artist is the raw super-subject. If there is no subject as Althusser claims, and if the subject has no unique qualities, then the artist cannot be. In the present climate the isolated certainties which propel each individual vision must operate separately from and with indifference and opposition to, the depreciation of the world in which he lives.

An artist starts from an excitement. Hugo, writing of Baudelaire, called it a 'frisson' and jazz musicians called it 'cookin'. Romantic poets call it 'inspiration' and ancients poets believed it came from divine beings they called 'muses'. The descriptions of the way in which inspiration comes to an artist unbidden, as sexual excitement comes unbidden, is repeated in different cultural arenas throughout history from the shaman who talks in tongues to the Japanese calligrapher waiting for the 'chi' and on to D. H. Lawrence proclaiming 'Not I but the wind that blows through me'. The frisson is fugitive, as fugitive as an erection. It intensifies and then it fades. If it is to be fished out of the stream of consciousness and stabilised an artefact must be made which embodies it and generates it to other people. Any good artist knows when his work has trapped his excitement, just as an excited lover knows if he has an erection. Bad artists will scrap their initial excitement for an effect which is more easily achieved, or they will deceive themselves and accept an imperfect botching of materials whereby transmission of the frisson is weak or approximate.

... recognising mastery ... (Jazz Audience Savoy Ballroom, Harlem. George Rosenthal)

In presenting or performing his work an artist knows that his audience, when he has one, divides into at least five main groups.

Firstly there are those who reject the work because they are insufficiently sensitive to experience the frisson.

Secondly there are those who experience the excitement and declare the work to be slight, having passed beyond this stage of inspiration to a broader and more advanced level.

Thirdly there are those who hear and enjoy the work, recognising mastery.

Fourthly there are those who do not experience the frisson but who recognise, from various characteristics of the work, that there are special qualities here which will reward a longer perusal.

Fifthly there are those who believe that the appreciation of art brings with it an aura of higher awareness which is a means to status and power. These people watch closely the reactions of critics and commentators whose sensitivity is acknowledged and copy them. The more esoteric the art, the higher the kudos.

Good artists turn away from the debate in which all aesthetic qualities are held to be equal and comparable because their work along these lines pragmatically contradicts the values that are imposed by those who study the means of art instead of reading the implementation of those means. They are able to recognise among the speakers too many who are claiming and, indeed, commanding credibility, who are insensitive to the properties of what they are discussing. The Cardiff post-modernist who declares *Eastenders* to be as good as Shakespeare's plays is not voicing an interesting valid opinion. He is not even putting forward a possibility. He is wrong and artists know it. Everywhere they tacitly register their recognitions of quality even in the midst of their inability or disinclination to discuss it. The artist of achievement is treated with deference and respect by other artists. The innovators and transgressors are circled warily. The inept are ruthlessly cut dead. The respected critic is feared. The appreciative audience is loved. The unappreciative is ruthlessly ignored. The critical arena is currently thronged with critics and self-appointed artists who belong to the category of the unappreciative.

Many of these critics come from training in art history or in cultural studies, areas in which Structuralism was readily embraced. Their skills of evaluation and their standards of judgement are different from those required to assess the aesthetic strength of art. Historians judge authenticity and fall prone to a presupposition that the new cannot be assessed and that true value may only be accorded to recognised masters whose reputations have stood the test of a century at least. Students of culture do not judge. They merely read art as part of the composite of culture in which it emerged. It is easier to map history when change is removed from the hands of marauding individuals; it is easier to analyse culture when it cannot be subverted.

Since artists, particularly the poets, bestowed upon their inspiration the godly personification of a muse, they have not thought of themselves as reflecting, personifying or even belonging to their age. Their work, originally addressed to the gods, not to posterity, attempts a significance beyond the contemporary. As philosophers make heretofore unheard analyses of what existence is, as scientists reveal facts about matter and space not previously known, so artists perpetually explore and extend what is available to human sensibility, to the emotions and to the senses. All three professions, philosophy, science and art, are attempting eventually to postulate information that was not previously on the agenda and are coining terms to notate what they postulate. Consequently they cannot be said to belong to a synthesis of previously digested information. Darwin did not belong to Victorian Christian Europe. He sprang from it, distanced himself from it and redirected it. So did Nietzsche. So did Cézanne, Brontë, Turner, Baudelaire and Debussy.

Philosophers and scientists find their information with their brains. Artists find their information with their senses. In the understanding of a nettle you start with the sting. After being stung you may dissect the plant and analyse the toxin. Artists are concerned with the sting only. They remain in the situation of the infant exploring a new world with lips and fingertips, ears and eyes, astounded by new radiances, new concatenations, tortured by new injuries, excited by new pleasure. Pleasure and desire are indeed the cutting edges of an artist's skill which is why so many artists address themselves to pleasure as though it were more than just a pastime. For artists pleasure is work, a duty not to be shirked.

Professional philosophers, scientists and artists do not lie for money. If they change their product for money they usually take pains to advertise their corruption so that it is not confused with their work. If they take money to produce what someone else requires them to produce for power or for monetary gain, they have probably ceased to be philosophers and scientists. They have, temporarily at least, certainly ceased to be artists.

Hitler by Heinrich Knirr, 1937.
Imperial War Museum, London

Hitler did not order what he required from Wagner, Nietzsche or Heidegger. He took something from each but he did not control the product. Two of them were dead anyway, as intellectuals often are when society takes an interest. The artists Hitler did control were emasculated and their work is no longer of use. The CIA did not commission the paintings of Pollock, De Kooning and Motherwell. They took something from each and deployed it for their own purpose but they had no part in the making of the works. Propagandists, entertainers, decorators, designers and advertisers are very, very unlikely to be artists in the real sense. If they are artists as the propagandist Heartfield was, as the entertainer Louis Armstrong was, they are artists by the right of qualities other than those defined and controlled by the popular demand they serve. The wit and pungency of Heartfield's juxtapositions will resonate in any society where there is a recognition of referential dissonance and a hatred of tyranny. Louis Armstrong's cuddly stereotype so despised by young black people today, sang with harmonic overtones and a staccato placing of notes and phrases, with guttural slurs that carried the passions of the heart into the sounds, the fluids and the substances of the body as no genre blues singer has ever done. His trumpet flights establish a mode of soaring joy which takes place in the physical world with no self-defeating conditions of spirituality or escape. Both are artists by right of their exploratory aesthetics which carry them beyond their time, dragging their society with them. If society is to appropriate art for its own purposes it must nullify the qualities that make it art.

Albert Janusch. Water Sports 1936.
If Society is to appropriate art for its own purposes ...

A. Samokhalov
Kirov at the sports parade 1935.

Whatever French philosophers may say about them, artists believe that they are advancing the human lot. Because they believe this they are prepared to tolerate cruel poverty, total incomprehension, accusations of madness, isolation from their uncomprehending loved ones and frequently persecution. Currently they seem to cheerfully ignore having been declared impossible. It would be interesting to hear how the present crop of self-styled artists who so unabashedly embrace the capitalist ideology can deal with the way Russian artists worked for decades in the face of Soviet control, how the artists of Europe sustained forced expatriation fleeing Hitler, how Picasso painted Guernica in defiance of Hitler and Franco, or how artists struggled against the constriction of the Church for centuries. Some of them may be sophisticated enough to claim that such acts of heroic dedication constitute the pathetic acceptance of a role in the mythology of bourgeois individualist stereotypes but that would require Marxist roots which they clearly lack.

The Structuralist belief in the historical impotence of the individual feeds an idle public the news it wants to hear. If these objects, these scribblings, these disruptive musical works cannot have consequences in the shaping of events what are they? Firstly they are the product of the culture, not its determinant. Lacking any particular practical use, they are decoration, empty emblems of status for those who can pay prices known to be high; the detritus of society, curiosities, bric-a-brac, some of which become collectable like the personal possessions of celebrities, cigarette cards or redundant postage stamps. Stripped of importance, they no longer challenge comprehension. No-one need feel any more that something is going on that they don't understand and about which they were not consulted. This change is readily embraced because it fits in with society's vengeful rejection of the egghead and capitalism's claim to ethical credibility on egalitarian grounds. The rejection has been empowered to go beyond a mere statement of 'We don't want this pretentious crap' to 'This pretentious crap was never what it cracked itself up to be anyway.'

My book attempts to correct this rejection. Humanity is condemned to develop whether it wants to or not. This being the case it had best develop along desirable lines, ethical lines which ensure that the vehicle of society may traverse lands where our children and grandchildren will be happy to find themselves. In the face of vileness bequeathed to us by our parents we have developed a distrust of the steering wheel and of anyone who chooses to man it. A central element in the rejection of Modernism and the historicity that went with it is a hope that dismantling progressive programmes will grant humanity a non-specific freedom in which to drift aimlessly, guided only by half-hearted impulses that have been rigorously drained of love, passion and conviction, those tedious old tyrants of the blood. The sad fact is that progress dismantled leaves a playground where all waters are shallow and there are no goals. When those who reveal new truths are disregarded, the psychopath steps in. The old-fashioned psychopaths are no longer restrained by firm ethical convictions. All brutal self-interest is licensed and Mammon, whose modern form is consumer capitalism, inspires psychopathy on a corporate scale. Society does violence to humanity.

Middlesex. 1995.

In Number 3 of the old film studios at Pinewood, corridors run down the sides of each hangar where actors wait between shots. While the crew lay tracks, knock up new structures, set props, adjust lights, tired people of all ages, suddenly absurd in their costumes, stripped of the animation they contrive when the Director shouts 'Action!' slop around on floppy broken-backed sofas, nuzzling tepid Polystyrene cups of tea and coffee, swilling plastic bottles of expensive water, poring over publications that betray the sad stupidity that lies behind many a sparkling personality of the lounge lozenge.

Periodically they drift to the tea urn on its trolley and thumb through what's left on the biscuit tray. Actors, like air travellers, stay docile if regularly and continuously fed.

At the end of the wall steep steps lead into a toilet. Along the wall hang paintings. They were bought in the days when Rank Studios were at the peak of their short-lived ambition, when Lockwood, Roc, Grainger, Attenborough et al were drawing level with the Hollywood greats, because this was also a time of optimism in British painting. Heron, Wynter, Lanyon and Frost were establishing a centre of high creativity in St. Ives where the Nicolsons were already ensconced. Annually the country's art students contributed to the huge, varied and swiftly changing Young Contemporaries exhibition, where at least five competitive directions in art vied for prominence. The paintings in the corridor look as though they have been purchased at the Young Contemporaries and hung there to enhance the idle moments of film people.

'Are these props?' asks the leading man, stooping to read something someone has scrawled on one of them in Biro. On another someone has chalked TEA with an arrow pointing towards the urn.

'What?' asks the leading lady.

'These paintings.'

'What paintings?' she says.

3.   THE ART JOB

> We cannot believe in art if we do not believe in some
> kind of unchanging attitude towards, or timeless
> standards of, what is beautiful, what is important, and
> what is essential in life.
>
> Sol Le Witt.

London, 1950.

The twenty-first is a daring one. Bunny didn't want boring old Victor Sylvester with all those waltzes and sambas and things. She's got awfully fond of this jazz music stuff – you know, all the instruments are playing different things at the same time. So we all tromped along to the Savoy to listen. Jolly vigorous stuff. Hot cha cha daddy-o!

The future of England is stomping glassy eyed all over the dance floor. The number is Wild Man Blues and the bass player is taking the breaks. During one of the breaks a sweaty and bespectacled scion grabs the PA mike and says 'Okay everyone! Happy Birthday to Bunny!' He leads an off-key version of Twenty One Today while the band tries to finish Wild Man Blues.

The trombonist, a taciturn unsmiling Yorkshireman, leads the band into the next number, an eloquent slow version of Mood Indigo. He stands to take his solo which he builds, phrase by phrase, as a builder might build a tower, brick by brick. While he is playing another young man leaps on stage and taps him on the shoulder. 'I say,' he shouts in the trombonist's ear, 'Could you play Twelfth Street Rag? You know – ' He commences to sing Twelfth Street Rag in case the trombonist doesn't know it. The solo is finished to the young man's bewilderment. Puzzled, he returns to the dance floor. 'They just do as they please,' he cries.

The number winds up.

'Peasants,' the trombonist mutters to the trumpet player. 'Real fuckin' peasants.'

Artists, and particularly poets, have frequently disagreed with their employers. In religious societies, and that means all societies until very recently, God was believed to know what humanity did not yet know. So anybody committed to the extension of human awareness felt well advised to be on good terms with God. Indeed in many religious societies there was no gap between the artist and a representative of God. Artists were often priests and shamans. If not, they fell out with God's representatives whenever they wished to ignore, vary or alter the consensual dogma.

Similarly, although notoriously able to slide in and out of whoredom, artists can be seen to do this with an ill will, contradicting, ignoring, or subverting their patron's instructions down the ages. So often the story that enthralled the artists was a new truth, not the story the patron wanted to hear. A quick look at the lives of Leonardo Da Vinci, Mantegna, Rembrandt Van Rijn, Francesco Goya, Gerard Manley Hopkins, William Blake and Bix Beiderbecke will demonstrate this.

When religion lost its control in Europe in the face of the headlong advance of capitalist technology, artists were left as the only guardians of the ineffable. The speed with which they acknowledged this role was impressive. Previously the necessary dissent of creativity had been a personal and private affair for each individual artist who could box clever like Moliére or withdraw into an isolation that is dismissable as eccentric or insane, like Goya and Blake.

Within decades the eccentricity and/or insanity of the artist was mandatory, publicly performed as a life-style called bohemianism. Simultaneously artists formed groups, acknowledged collective titles like the Ancients, the Pre-Raphaelites, the Impressionists, the Symbolists, the Fauves, to declare their opposition to the main drift of the social economic consensus.

Along these routes artists struck contact, then broke again ... (André Breton, Diego Rivera, Leon Trotsky, Jacqueline Breton, Mexico 1938)

Ever since the Industrial Revolution, art's flirtation with technological advance was sporadic. Technology was, after all, the means by which Mammon had come to power with all its inability to understand aesthetics. Artists, however, research and make manifest their original information in a ludic workshop. Many of them couldn't keep their hands off new toys, from power-lathe to film, from photography to virtual reality, from typewriters to synthesisers. In withdrawal artists would repeatedly try to form pre-industrial communes like Gauguin or D.H. Lawrence. In crusade they would attempt to guide technology as William Morris and Walter Gropius did. In revolution they would try to seize technology, as Marinetti had, Bob Dylan did, as Alexander Trocchi wanted to.

Along these routes artists ran alongside breakaway religions like those of Madame Blavatski, Aleisteir Crowley and L. Ron Hubbard, the leftist politics of Prudhon and Marx, the libertarian philosophy of De Sade, Nietzsche and Sartre, the new science of psycho-analysis. All along these routes artists struck contact, then broke away again as soon as they were expected to obey the principles of each parallel discipline.

Artists know that the expansion of human awareness is perpetual. They know, therefore, that conclusions are never final. They must, in Marcuse's words 'break the monopoly of established reality (i.e. of those who established it) to *define* what is real.' Because of this, either militantly or secretly, they retain the ability to digress, divert or disobey. Obedient art is not possible.

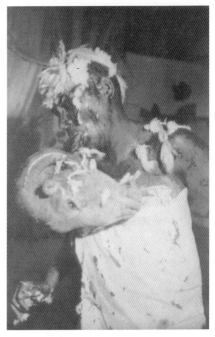

... no gap between the artist and the representative of God ... Sacrifice of a Ram. Voodoo cult.

London, 1992.
I am a little late – the Number 10 held up by traffic as thick as clotted porridge back as far as Selfridges. I walk up Portland Place and arrive at Broadcasting House sweating a little. I glance up at the Gill and, as always, recall the bon mot of the policeman sent up to measure the stone dick who wrote 'rude' in his notebook.

The man I am to meet is stooped, civilised and has a measured American voice that recalls Alan Lomax, Alistair Cooke and Earl Birney. He shakes me by the hand and suggests lunch and I gather he means lunch somewhere outside, not on BBC territory. It has been some time since I approached the British Communist Party in the hope of becoming a member. I had thought that the Communist Party had dissolved or, at any rate, much modified itself since Russia subsided in '89 but sitting in Aggie Falk's parlour in Hebden Bridge through which many worthwhile survivors inevitably pass in time, taking the wine and healing their wounds with humour and intelligence, I met two young people fatigued after a long night's electioneering. They were dressed modestly, free of the stylistic flak behind which stupidity conceals its pits and voids. Their conversation was clear, articulate and measured. They wanted no gestures or colours to impede the content of their modest talk. They were stunned, bewildered and bitter at

Kinnock's defeat and they were members of the British Communist Party, the BCP not the CPGB. Their party was live and strong, they said. If I felt as I did, that there is no time now for prevarication and fence-sitting, why did I not join? They would give me an address.

My application resulted in a phone call and a letter that spelled out to me that membership of the BCP was not so freely granted. Membership was not a passive thing in these days. Militant activity and preparedness for militant activity must be assured. Involvement of this kind was certainly what I felt to be my duty and was the reason I applied.

This is the culmination of decades of battling over priorities in the troubled ground between art and politics, long hours of trying to explain to CND representatives, Marxist representatives, Jeff Cloves, Roland Muldoon, Arthur Moyes, Albert Meltzer, Ted Kavanagh, Cliff Slaughter, Pam Brighton, anarchists and militants, many of them from the burgeoning leftist theatre of the early Sixties, CAST, Red Ladder, the Half Moon, that the good guys don't necessarily make good art and that good art is often created by Fascists.

Now this ambling charming American who works for the BBC Overseas Service and who looks as though he should be recording folk songs, ambles alongside me and we go into the first pub we come to which turns out not to be the most pleasant recreational spot in the Western World. Lunch is a half and a pasty for him. I have a pint and a melancholy cheese roll.

As I finish he says: 'Well Jeff, I hope this is the beginning of a real friendship. We must meet again when we have more time and enjoy a few pints and maybe some music. I must read some of your poetry and I'd love to see your visual work. You must realise that we value people like you very much but I'm afraid that I cannot recommend you for membership. You are most unlikely to be sufficiently obedient. Would you walk out of rehearsals to start a strike in Middlesborough?'

'That depends on a number of facts,' I say.

'Precisely,' he says. 'Unfortunately, we must claim absolute priority.'

PART TWO

THE FAILURE OF MILITANT ART

Dadaism demands the immediate expropriation of property (socialization) and the communal feeding of all: further the erection of cities of light, and gardens that will belong to society as a whole and prepare men for a state of freedom.

Dada Manifesto 1920.

Dave Tough used to read The American Mercury from cover to cover, especially the section called Americana where all the bluenose bigots and two-faced killjoys in this land-of-the-free got a going over they never forgot. That Mercury really got to be the Austin High Gang's Bible. It looked to us like Mencken was yelling a message in his magazine that we were trying to get across in our music; his words were practically lyrics to our hot jazz.

Mezz Mezzrow.

They want to hear *about*; they want to hear an objective conference on The Theatre and the Plague, and I want to give them the experience itself, so they will be terrified and awake. I want to awaken them. They do not realise *they are dead*.

Antonin Artaud.

1. SUBVERTING SABOTAGE.

In their vaguely defined and wildly varied opposition to the Twentieth Century, Western artists sustained two shocks which imposed upon them an unwelcome urgency. The first was the wanton destructiveness of the First World War, an incident which seemed to embody the fundamental evil of technology. The second was nuclear weapons.

The reaction to the '14–'18 holocaust was the formation of two influential organisations of militant artists — the Dadaists and the Surrealists.

The Dadaists — Tzara, Arp, Schwitters, Duchamp, Patchen — were wreckers. The Surrealists — Breton, Eluard, Ernst, Magritte, Bataille, Artaud, Buuel — attempted an alternative reality. Much has been written by or about both movements so this discussion here must confine itself to those elements which fed the sequence of events leading to our present cultural bankruptcy. The understanding of our present emergency results from understanding the subtle way in which Mammon changed his face and his language to encompass the vocabulary of Dada and Surrealism. Mammon used his anatomy of demonised money to dismantle the Nineteenth Century shibboleths of power, the Government, the aristocracy and the Church, where leftist militancy had failed; and Mammon deployed the language of Dada and Surrealism as décor when sabotage had been intended, along with swastikas, union jacks, and antique uniforms. A new group of revolutionary capitalists over-ran both the old establishment and its opposition, rubbishing the first and playing in the detritus of the second.

This play was facilitated by the Structuralists. A psychological missile like Duchamp's urinal had been disarmed by being redefined as a collectable curiosity. It could now be hung in a dwelling place as shell cases could be placed on mantelpieces or pistols used as paper-weights. Nonetheless a Duchamp or an Arp would retain something of the uncomfortable alienating quality of its

... young artists in one of the temples of sacredness ...
The constructivist-dadaist congress in Weimar 1922.

original militancy.   Post-Modern artists learned how to achieve a neutral outrageousness, a contravention so bland and so slickly produced it took its place passively in the interior, with no history of unease to intrude into the ambience of the room's usage.

A gathering of surrealists, 1924. Standing left to right: Charles Baron, Raymond Queneau, Pierre Naville, André Breton, J.A Boiffard, Giorgio de Chirico, Roger Vitrac, Paul Eluard, Phillipe Soupault, Robert Desnos, Louis Aragon. Seated Left to right: Simone Breton, Max Morise, Mick Soupault

But the Structuralists had a fascination with both Dada and Surrealism.   They were, after all, Parisian, and Paris has been the platform of the brilliant flaneur for some time.   From Baudelaire to Baudrillard there is a perceptible continuum, a constant tradition of intellectual audacity in which nihilism is writ large.   'Le Grand Maulne', the arrogant and delinquent schoolboy lover of Fournier's classic novel, was a role-model lending a lot to Jarry, Jacob, Tzara, Aragon, Breton, Genet, Prévert, Eluard.   Perhaps going back as far as Villon, to claim main credibility in Paris it was necessary to be a naughty boy, or at least stand near one as Sartre stood near Genet.   Intellectuals finding themselves in the comparative respectability of the university surely felt themselves compelled to carry out their discipline whether it be psychology (Lacan), literature (Derrida), or semiology (Barthes) in a destructive way that denied the viability of thought.   Polemic performed with a boulevard raconteur's wit, speed and elegance, whirled itself into such convoluted knots of opacity that its opacity became impossible to deny and even a quality to pursue.   Eventually Derrida claimed that there was only the text, reduced to a kind of coasting within the tide of events of the culture.   He claimed that the text wrote the author, finding, in its auto-pilot impetus, sense, half-sense or nonsense which then redefined ('dissolved') the writer.   When asked whether his work was to be regarded as literature or philosophy he replied with a typical oxymoronic knot:

'I will say that my texts belong neither to the "philosophical" register nor to the "literary" register.   Thereby they communicate or so I hope at least, with other texts that, having operated a certain rupture, can be called 'philosophical' or 'literary' only according to a kind of paleonomy: the question of *paleonomy*:   what is the *strategic* necessity (and why do we still call strategic an operation that in the last analysis refuses to be governed by a teleo-eschatalogical horizon?   Up to what point is this refusal possible and how does it *negotiate* its effects?   Why must it negotiate these effects, including the effect of this why itself?   *Why* does *strategy* refer to the play of the stratagem rather than to the hierarchical organisation of the means and the ends? etc.

Raku Pot by Charles Bound

Lavender Mist 1 by Jackson Pollock 1950

These questions will not be quickly reduced.), what then is the "strategic" necessity that requires the occasional maintenance of an *old name* in order to launch a new concept.' The invalid categories of literature and philosophy could best be deconstructed by writing which denied the properties of either. There was not literature and there was not philosophy. There was only writing.

The proximity of this language-attitude to that of the accidental word-scrambles of Dada (when Tzara amongst others made poems by shaking up chopped-up newspapers in a bag), the drive of all Dada manifestos towards explosive gibberish, Breton's surrealist automatism (trance-writing with the controlling intellect as far as possible nullified) and Artaud's schizophrenic hospital scribble, is so close it becomes embarrassing, so clearly does it betray the professor's wish to be an artist. Barthes had, after all, advised his peers: 'Don't talk about it. Do it.'

Truth is the casualty here because a fundamental existential reading has not been made by the Structuralists. Art deliberately abandons control in order to find that which may not be found by a mind guided according to learned or habitual modes of perception. Every artist knows that it is impossible to paint a blot. The Raku potters and carvers of Japan knew it was impossible to carve or model a convincing fracture. Breton knew that if the unconscious mind must be deployed the conscious mind must be circumvented. The authentic quality, beauty, dynamic of the uncontrolled was the goal and its authenticity, so obviously absent when faked, was the truth. Dada displayed the same fracture in polemic as if to pragmatically demonstrate what they were about. Surrealists were totally unambiguous in their polemic, outlining their principle with the savage clarity of a police announcement. The truth that Structuralism was anxious to explore was that put forward but not demonstrated by Levi-Strauss, Chomsky and Saussure, that the culture determines the whole of every individual's behaviour, that language is the genetic continuum of the culture bearing humanity forward to a destiny in which the mind takes no initiative. This pursuit was uncomfortable because the situation of a professional thinker arguing that thought had no power over language pragmatically contradicted the thinker's contention. If writing was to be granted sovereignty, then the writer must resign from his own continuing work.

What is not understood is that in art the resignation of the subject is temporary. He returns to his accidents whether he be John Cage, Jackson Pollock, Wols or William Burroughs, and he selects, moulds, enhances and often places them in a work in which they interlock with passages of impeccable skilled control. Their truth lies in their effect and those who achieve the effect do so because, like the four names above, they are very fine artists.

But philosophy doesn't pragmatically demonstrate its truth by the effectiveness of its forms. It deploys language in an analytic, communicative way. Ambiguity is its enemy. Display sabotages it. When it grants language its autonomy it resigns without sidestepping into the alternative course of innovation and leaves not a panoply of excitement and delight but a lame void. The reasoner has attempted the music but he hasn't the ear. Why should he have? How could he have? Is the cartographer a painter?

2.   SABOTAGE BY FOUND OBJECT

> Surrealism is based on the belief in the superior reality in certain forms of association heretofore neglected, in the omnipotence of the dream, the disinterested play of thought. It leads to the permanent destruction of all the other psychic mechanisms and to the substitution for them in the solution to the principal problems in life.
>
> André Breton.

The Dadaists were infantile. The word itself – Dada - meaning hobby horse was found at random by sticking a pin in a French dictionary. They saw the entire structure of society, the things it held sacred, the things it despised, its pantheon of heroes, saints and criminals, disgraced by the carnage all around. As young artists they found themselves in one of the temples of sacredness, an area in which the voices of statesmen would have been hushed and deferential as they had once been in cathedrals. In the cathedral of art Dada artists thought the least they could do was shit on the altar. They did this by holding exhibitions in which artefacts of beauty and high skill were replaced with banal household objects. They gave readings in which they replaced the high truth of poetry with chopped up fragments of newspapers. They gave concerts in which music was replaced by noise. They fully deployed a new element in the artist's toolbox, the *objét trouvé*, the found object, and being artists, they deployed it beautifully. Kurt Schwitters pasted his rubbish together with the quiet grandeur of a Chardin. Duchamp mounted his bike wheel and his urinal with the elegant nicety of an engineer's maquette.

... The elegant nicety of an engineer's maquette ...
(Marcel Duchamp. Bicycle Wheel 1913)

So there was a subtext to the outrage and the subversion of Dada. Whilst tearing down the authoritarian *noblesse* of fine art they were revealing the quiet beauty of all visible, audible things. When Duchamp instructed us to use a Rembrandt as an ironing board he was not just farting in the holy silence

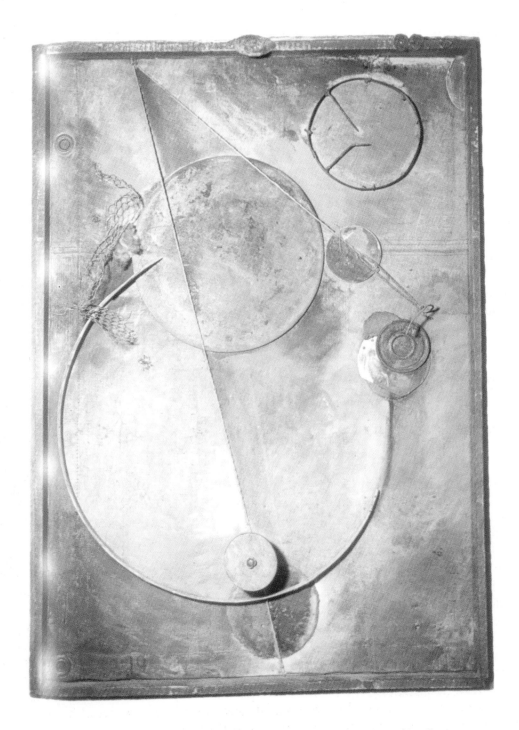

... Kurt Schwitters pasted his rubbish together with the quiet grandeur of a Chardin ...

surrounding the Dutch master. He was also giving a quiet blessing to the ironing board. When Schwitters joined his bus tickets and sink brushes together he did it with a loving eye to their echoing colours and forms. Beauty, this sub-text declared, is obscured by the ballyhoo of cultural reverence. Only the infant can taste it fresh. Dada, in its infantilism, has revealed the secret universality of beauty. Unknowingly they had strayed into Zen Buddhism.

It was this sub-text which Buddhist composer John Cage and beatnik painters Rauschenberg and Jim Dine took from Dada and it was thus that they deployed sound objects and found objects. The Dadaists were secretly and finally aesthetic. All things are beautiful, they demonstrated. He who reveals this is as much an artist as he who can draw like Raphael or scan like Homer. It required no more training or skill than that possessed by a little child.

The curious flowering of interest in the daubs of small children and the work of untrained artists called naives followed immediately, lubricated by the polemic of Roland Penrose, Herbert Read and Marian Richardson. Between the wars there was a profound distrust on the part of the best thinkers, of the mature, the civilised and the socially or industrially determined, and there was a belated embrace for creativity that precluded or altogether evaded social conditioning.

The surrealists despised aesthetics. Beautiful was not a word they used much but erotic was a word they used a lot. Their work was depictive, which is to say that it took place around the subject matter. The work itself was not to be enjoyed. The painting and the poem advertised the pleasures of sex, liberty and transgression. Surrealists also used *objéts trouvé*.

The first appearance of the *objét trouvé* was literary. It appeared in the remarkable extended prose-poem by Lautréamont some thirty years before either the Dada or Surrealist movements. Lautréamont speaks of the 'chance meeting between an umbrella and a sewing machine on the operating table.' Certainly these are literary images, not the actual objects, but when the objects are assembled by a sculptor their juxtaposition could resonate in a way that was identical to the way in which found objects resonated in surrealist writing.

Objects in Surrealism have the secret significance which Freud gave them in his analysis of dreams, although Lautréamont's scenario appeared a significant time before Freud's analyses. They are euphemisms for the unthinkable, from the obvious equivalents between chimneys and penises to the more obscure resonances of crutches, rotting watermelons, and railway engines. Surrealist found-objects are objects charged with associative magic. They are fetishes working like the bric-a-brac of the witch doctor or the sexual obsessive. They detonate a world of consequence, power and some dread in human response and they are not in the least infantile. The old fashioned aesthetic values of shape, colour, texture and space are not acknowledged by the Surrealist. Surrealist *objéts trouvés* are agents of birth, sex, power, pain and death. They assault the public equilibrium.

Untitled (bath) Rachel Whiteread
... post-modern use of objets trouvés ...

Object (Luncheon in Fur) Meret Oppenheim 1936
... surrealist use of objets trouvés ...

Saddle and handlebars bull. Picasso
... a cubists use of objets trouvés ...

... a celebration of consumerism not a subversion ...
(Brillo Boxes Andy Warhol 1964)
... a pop use of objets trouvés ...

Both movements were subversive. Language was scrambled or set on auto-pilot in order to steal it back from propagandists and those whose reasoning formed the cornerstones of an increasingly self-destructive society. *Objéts trouvés*, so often found among the bric-a-brac of that society were, like language, filched out of the commercial location and deployed as aesthetic form or erotic metaphor.

The development of consumer bric-a-brac appearing in the later Pop Art, although often held to be a continuation of Dada and Surrealism, was existentially different. Although appearances and material were similar, even identical, their use was a celebration of consumerism, not a subversion.

3. MAMMON RULES O.K.

> The dominant stream now is more about looseness
> and mobility and things being very casually made, or
> hardly ever appearing to have been made at all, and
> being close to the ephemera of pop culture.
>
> Matthew Colling.

The Surrealist assault on society was not as nihilistic as the Dada onslaught. Surrealism means a deeper reality, the search for it, the belief in it and the intention of replacing the world's consensual materialism with a spectrum of desire, ecstasy and imagination by a mental and cultural revolution. The Surrealists acknowledged and flirted with Marxism, anarchism and Freudianism.

For both Dadaists and Surrealists eccentricity, isolation, disobedience and bohemianism, were not enough. The separation and freedom which artists had automatically assumed over the centuries was now a militant standpoint from which the world must be immediately transformed.

The surviving importance of the trained artist's eye in the aesthetics of Dada, the vital importance of the ability to evoke and juxtapose acutely vivid metaphoric images in the psycho-subversion of Surrealism, were qualities still necessitating considerable artistic vision and skill. Within these two militant schools, both of which loathed and eschewed traditional standards of critical evaluation, it is still no matter of argument that Kurt Schwitters was a great Dadaist and Richard Huelsenbecke was not, or that Max Ernst was a great Surrealist and Conroy Maddox is not. They were artists and their comparable achievements are facts, not variable notions.

Nonetheless, so radically had art developed by now that the public had no way of applying their old evaluative yardsticks of realism, narrative, and sweetness of harmony. To the public eye art had been deskilled. It took no rigorous drawing training to assemble junk. It took no training in the metre and syntax of the classics to notate the subconscious. It took no instrumental training to join in the making of atonal sound-patterns. Anybody could do it as, indeed, the anarchist egalitarians rejoiced in pointing out for some time. Douanier Rousseau was as good as Braque, Alfred Wallis was as good as Ben Nicholson. Creativity was a human faculty and a human right. The fact that the whole yardstick of quality could be set against the inalienable rights of each individual seemed a powerful weapon in any programme of cultural revolution that intended the overthrow of a vertical social structure. 'Saints have been kissing lepers,' said R.D. Laing in the Sixties. 'It is time the leper kissed the saint.'

It was certainly time for the criminal to be granted his sainthood. Sartre sanctified the thief Genet. Norman Mailer hailed the psychopath as saviour.

It was also time for artists to move out of their studios and involve the public in work which no longer required skill. John Fox and Boris Howarth took their Welfare State performance tribe into the towns of Lancashire and Cumberland, determined to turn art into carnival and carnival into art. Tim Jones, working with the Open University, showed students how to make and display their own body prints. Cornelius Cardew, the Communist composer, initiated his Scratch Orchestra, a travelling atonal jam session in which all were invited to participate.

Brian Eno organised the Portsmouth Symphonia in which untrained musicians attempted to perform the work of the classic composers. These and many other artists redefined the studio as the street, handing the tools and the materials over to the public, including waiters. The community, a word much in use amongst these activists, had lost its cultural focus in the chaos of cultural mixings, inputs and evacuations, alienated, it was argued, by exploitative media technology. Folk forms, for long the natural creativity of communities, had only survived as the carrot in the camera-snapping tourist industry — Morris dancers and well-dressing.

The community and the creative-play-shamans were too late. The only people who wanted to play were other artists and informed sympathisers who were themselves conversant with and supportive of the strategy. The community, such as it was still a possibility, was already mesmerised by Rock and Roll, soap fiction and the oncoming tidal wave of computer developments. Community games and post-Dada carnival were all very well but increasingly they involved the uneasy proximity of strangers, with their infections, their embarrassments, their occasional violence and, worst of all, their reality. Delusion was becoming as convincing as empirical reality, with joys that were maybe less profound than those of love and art, but which carried less risk.

People were coming to maturity infinitely better acquainted with the harmless-because-fictitious inhabitants of *Coronation Street* and *Emmerdale Farm* and when the Internet arrived individuals could not only receive fiction; they could transmit their

... joys that were maybe less profound than those of love and art but which carried less risk ...
The TV age.

own. Everyman could dissolve himself and replace himself with Vlad the Impaler. Community artists could go back to their studios and rediscover art which, in its intensity, its power and poetic verity, had become somewhat diluted. The disintegrated community had, indeed, created a vacuum into which Mammon had moved with alacrity, hypnotising everybody with its new toys and with its new, impenetrable monopolies.

Nonetheless an attempt was made for the easy to replace the difficult, for the unskilled and insensitive to usurp the concert platform and for the philosophers and thinkers to dismantle all structures of argument that might hinder the opening of the floodgate.

The rationale for this scrapping of criteria in the Sixties and Seventies was the peril of continuing the existing social structure made manifest by the stockpiling of nuclear weapons. In 1945 the opposition between artists and the socio-economic establishment ceased to be a matter of dislike, debate, dissent, disapproval, even revolution. It became a matter of the continuation or termination of the human race on earth and so it remained, with Russian nuclear weapons nose-to-nose with American nuclear weapons, for forty-five years.

Now that the High Noon scenario has relaxed, with Russia's back-down and America's seemingly effortless triumph, it's possible for those of us who spent most of our adult lives in four-and-a-half decades of confrontation to look back and see how crucially discoloured our lives became under that quiet unrelenting terror. How we were harmed by the heavy probability, not only of one's own premature death, but of the self-termination of humanity. So many structures and practices were cast into doubt that are fundamental to human benevolence and growth: love, children, family, law, government, history, skill and permanence. Some of these structures we attacked virulently and naively, some we only maintained half-heartedly. We were diseased. Symptoms of this disease are now open to objective examination a decade after the Soviet collapse. The militant artists were feeble and the '68 revolution was a mere tantrum. Nonetheless even Peregrine Worsthorne now concedes that the deterrent argument was blind, irresponsible and criminally dangerous. There were, after all, round-the-clock bomb-carrying planes in the air for forty five years, to ensure that the opponents equalled one another, even in the matter of a last strike on an already uninhabitable world. Even now that the duellists have retired from the immediate arena they have not yet disarmed. Indeed their weapons have proliferated and there is nothing as yet to prevent a nose-to-nose duelling situation re-emerging, maybe in the middle-east, or as it has evolved recently between India and Pakistan.

So although we were half mad the cry was not entirely misguided when philosophers, scientists, artists and anybody from all parts of the industrial world who specialised in truth, howled for immediate action to dismantle a society which intended mutual suicide.

Artists, led by the American beat writers Allen Ginsberg, Kerouac and William Burroughs, and the Parisian group of post-Surrealists, the Situationists, led by Guy Debord, Alex Trocchi, Ralph Rumney and Raoul Vaneigem, formed an international underground whose accumulative effect attempted that total transformation of consciousness which had been the objective of Surrealism. They primed a social revolution which became suddenly urgent, went off at half-cock in 1968, and failed. The goal of an international cultural consensus based on ecstasy, vision and common humanity was not achieved. Universal sexual joy was not achieved. Poverty, suffering and human squalor remained. War continued sporadically. People continued to print, use, and squabble over money. The revolutionaries floundered for ten years flirting with ill-informed Marxism, dealing with the ethical void left by the dissolved codes of marriage and family cohesion, developing new and uncontrollable diseases in a field of unprecedented universal promiscuity, finding inconsequential protest activities to occupy them once the protest against nuclear weapons and state oppression had failed, developing a growing reliance on the charity of the triumphant enemy, the state, in National Assistance, Social Security and Welfare handouts, drowning in epidemics of implosive drug use.

By 1980 the cultivation of the global consciousness had turned into the cultivation of the self by fashion, life-style and diet, while nobody knew what was good any more as opposed to bad, or vital as opposed to feeble. Nobody knew who the artists were any more unless they were told, so there was no-one to whom to turn when Mammon invaded and destroyed both the diseased forces of revolution and the out-dated forces of oppression.

PART THREE

UNDER THE ROCK AND ROLL DOME

Art is a subsidiary of the pop music industry. Or at least it should be if it is to have real meaning and currency in the modern world.

Waldemar Januszczak.

1. THE ROCK PLOY

The first measure the militant artists took in the years leading up to '68 was to climb out of their ivory towers and their bohemian ghettos to move in on the popular culture, in on entertainment, fashion, the media, all of which were commercially motivated and commercially controlled. Those artists who came together in a spontaneous action to obviate nuclear suicide had little doubt that the forces of Mammon and the forces of militarism were one. The culture must be wrested from Mammon and be used as a vehicle for instant universal higher awareness. Further, they realised that the new vision that art pursued perpetually was the necessary basis for any belief in the value of the continuation of human life on the planet. With total liberal egalitarianism they embraced the belief common to Marxism and anarchism, that humanity was cut off from art, its awareness, its vision, its depth, height, joy and crucial despair, because it had become stupefied by exploitation, and numbed by industrial labour that ignored and killed off the natural skills, by underpaying which limited the pleasure range, and by overwork which left no time for mental, spiritual or creative life.

Before the nuclear emergency there seemed time for art to seep through into the culture until its social benefit was enjoyed, until such time, as it were, that the Impressionist daub that caused a riot in 1870 found its way as far as the biscuit tin, the calendar and the life-style. Suddenly we were no longer dealing with social benefit. We were dealing with the need for instant survival. If people were to understand why it was important for their species to remain on the planet, there was no time for the health of the aesthetic to filter into the culture. It had to be inoculated into the culture immediately, by infiltration, subversion, and force if need be.

Rock and Roll presented itself as an aspect of the popular culture that was more likely to be receptive to intervention than movies or radio serials. It was an idiom addressing itself to young people, largely played by young people. It already carried with it a content of non-specific rebellion, chiefly against sexual restraint. Young people seemed exceptionally approachable because they were undeceived. As they came to puberty, generation by generation, they seemed to arrive with a detailed contempt for materialism, property, snobbery, discipline, respectability, frigidity, prudery and war. They appropriated Rock and Roll, its stars, its concerts, its paraphernalia, as a focal structure through which they could put cultural distance between themselves and the parent generation.

Artists, with their minority following (and this included jazz artists who never had any connection with Rock and Roll, even as a source for Rock and Roll) had never

47

A whole class of young people had started to behave as though they believed their future to be worthless ...

... music with tin-roof harmonics and a gospel hall back-beat ... (Jerry Lee Lewis)

Gene Vincent

... The fuck and run delinquent with a secret sorrow and a heart of shot gold ... (Elvis Presley, Don Craven 1958)

previously had any interest in Rock and Roll. Indeed the word 'commercial' was the most disparaging term of condemnation in jazz, and indeed in the whole of art, marking the corrupt and the meretricious off from the creative and the dedicated. Rock and Roll was a part of the commercial popular culture, together with fashion, comics, Tin Pan Alley, Hollywood, part of the very mind-stultifying pap which industry provided in order to keep the workers stupid and happy. It was, in fact, a considerable regression, even in the popular mode, a technologically inflated extension of folk forms, which leapfrogged the sophisticated songs of the musical comedy, the ornate and richly modulated structures of George Gershwin, Jerome Kern and Irving Berlin, and arrived centre-stage with two or three chords, instrumentation confined to guitars, drums and keyboards, a style of diluted blues-singing and enough sound technology to plaster over the defects.

When artists focused their attention on it Rock and Roll was an idiom directed at the white American college and high school audience, a social group that was already beginning to sanctify its deviants. Amidst the hot rod drivers in their blue jeans and bobby sox there was a strong feckless fashion for risk and self destruction. A whole class of young people had started to behave as though they had started to believe their future to be worthless or maybe simply not likely to arrive, and Rock and Roll was eventually the music of those millions who identified with James Dean's character in *Rebel Without A Cause*, of Marvin's and Brando's characters in *The Wild Ones*. The debate goes on about the degree to which these characters embodied an existing tendency or sparked off a new one. The stereotypes of Gene Vincent, Terry Dean, Eddie Cochran, Billy Fury, Adam Faith, Duane Eddy and the great god Elvis, with their DA haircuts, slanted caps, leather jerkins, became the models for gathering generations of young people who hadn't the acumen to enjoy the high separation obtained through art. The fuck-and-run delinquent with a secret sorrow and a heart of shot gold became the charismatic image revered by the young middle class as the young people in the accurately detailed *Happy Days* TV sitcom revere The Fonz. You didn't have to read Sartre's *Being and Nothingness* any more to step out of society. You didn't have to follow the contorted harmonic progressions of Arnold Schoenberg, Thelonius Monk or Charlie Parker. You didn't have to take in the paint slingers and their apologist Clement Greenberg. Here was music with tin-roof-chapel harmonies and a gospel-hall back beat that spelled out the simple goals of freedom, disobedience, instant kicks and sex, unabashed physical, genital sex, casting a blind eye to reproductive restraints, demanding the Pill which had not yet arrived.

The beat poets, with their knowledge of Genet who was not yet published in either of the two bomb-owning nations, had a special poetic regard for wild youths in their own homosexual spectrum. The teen Rebel was as magical to them as he was to his junior high public. And now they could move in on his music and give him a Cause.

The effectiveness of the strategy can be seen easily by comparing the Beatles' *Rubber Soul* with the Beatles' *Revolver* and *Sergeant Pepper* albums. The transition from

Marilyn Monroe

Madonna
This system of selling the charisma of an individual
to the detriment and neglect of their integrity ...

the cynicism of *Norwegian Wood*, through the existential despair of *Day in The Life* to the political vision of later albums which included numbers like *Working Class Hero* and *Imagine* marks the intercession of the poet Allen Ginsberg, (introduced by poets Adrian Henri and Brian Patten), and performance artist Yoko Ono (introduced by art entrepreneur Barry Miles).

The transition of Bob Dylan from the role of folk-pixie pastiching Woodie Guthrie to the composer-performer of *A Hard Rain's Gonna Fall* and *The Times They Are A Changin'* betrayed, once again, the intercession of Allen Ginsberg.

The way in which poets, electronic composers and blues musicians like Jim Morrison, Frank Zappa, Jerry Garcia and Leonard Cohen moved onto the Rock and Roll bandstand indicated that the guitar and harmonica vocabulary of Chicago blues could extend the chordal strumming of the Fifties idols. Musicians who understood what Stockhausen had been doing with electronics in Cologne and what Morton Subotnik had been doing in San Francisco were prepared to set atonal sound in front of those wham-bang drumkits. The psychopathic cocksman got dreamy.

And the lyrics took on the throaty sexually explicit rawness of real blues, which introduced spiritual and even religious overtones and plumbed the detail of political unmentionables about power and war only previously found in angry Marxist poetry.

The artists had enlisted stars and some of them became stars. In doing so they imagined that they had seized a nerve centre of human communication. The danger escaped them that they ran the risk of being engulfed by their entry into a territory and system they had no way of understanding. A contempt for Mammon entails an underestimation of Mammon and certainly an ignorance about the complex networks of power that Mammon weaves and operates, off the centre stage of production and exploitation.

Stardom was a phenomenon of the Nineteenth Century popular theatre. In America, George B. Cohan, Lily Langtry and Amos 'N' Andy were stars. In Britain John McCormack, Clara Butt and Marie Lloyd. This system of selling the charisma of an individual to the detriment and neglect of their integrity, their intelligence, and their right to development and change, quickly translated to cinema and radio. It engulfed the singing of Sinatra and Crosby, and the trumpet playing of Harry James. It never touched the art of Roy Eldridge, Billie Holliday, Coleman Hawkins or Charlie Parker. These people were heroes to a sensitive minority. They stayed poor, free and vital.

2. THE DOME

London. 1969.
I have been working at Bradford for almost a year now. Back in London for a conflab with Mike Kustow I find myself in a pub near New End Hospital looking around for old pals.
'Hi Jeff,' says a man in denims with Afro hair.
'Hi,' I say, raking through my mind to identify him. I finally locate him as the musical editor of IT. IT, International Times, was the newspaper launched by Jim Haynes, Charles Marowitz and Tom McGrath as the organ of the spontaneous revolution. It started with a weekly cartoon by me which I contributed for nothing, assuming that in the free revolution all soldiers contributed their skills unpaid, deriving their livelihood elsewhere. This was no optimistic assumption. It seemed to me that payment, employment, even the consideration of profit, was a system inherently corrupt, laying the work open to compromise, censorship and political control.
Discovering that all other contributors were getting paid I withdrew the cartoon. Since then I'd had little contact with the paper. 'How are things at the office?' I ask.
He is now in conversation with another man of similar appearance. They are talking about record companies and contracts and the money offered the Pink Floyd for their American tour.
'What?' he says. 'Oh,' he says. 'Usual mess. I'm getting out. EMI have offered me better money writing sleeve notes.'
'Sleeve notes?' I say. 'What about the revolution?'
'Jeff,' he says pityingly, 'What revolution? You want a revolution, you have one Jeff.'

Stardom was the mode of Rock and Roll before the artists got there. It might be easy to take the star to a party, give him a ten inch spliff and breathe new wisdom into his ear. It was another thing to affect a similar persuasion on the shareholders, managers, public relations teams, lighting technicians, sound engineers, producers, directors and publicity networks that stand invisibly behind every spotlit god. Certainly all stars are pampered to the degree of enfeeblement. Certainly all stars may make their imperious demands and have them met, giving the illusion of their absolute control. But a star's control is the control of a thoroughbred racehorse that must be kept fed, fit and happy. No star organises the show any more than any horse lays the race track or sets the prices. They are primed into position and then, craftily, released into production. Mammon beams.

A main means of pointing Rock and Roll stars in a planet-saving direction was the introduction of drugs. They became a major instrument in Western society's divorce from truth. Without their widespread usage it seems possible that the way in which the Structuralists were pragmatically contradicting their contentions by arguing their own cases and signing texts which they held to be self-dictating, might have been evident to all. Indeed without drugs it seems possible that much of late Structuralist and Post-Modernist polemic might never have been written.

Drugs are receptive to, and productive of, information which is untrue. Unlike alcohol, users of which commonly know themselves to have been temporarily stupid whatever may be claimed about the *veritas* of *vino*, drugs produce in the user frequent claims of deeper understanding and higher truth. The drugs introduced in the Sixties were marijuana, amphetamine, cocaine, lysergic acid, barbiturates and heroin, more or less in that order of accumulating addictiveness.

Marijuana is insidiously dangerous because it seems to be harmless and even beneficial. It soothes the nerves and silences petty alarms. In fact, contrary to the strategy, it silences all alarms, even those which jangle when powerful opponents confront each other with nuclear weapons. It is a great postponer and it renders the user incapable of punctuality.

Amphetamines rob the mind of its correctives. They impose instant psychopathy, stripping patience, kindness and compassion even from the gentlest souls. They also induce paranoia. Users are prone to believe they are besieged by assassins.

Cocaine is similar to amphetamine. It speeds the mind, robbing it of the sympathetic communicative rhythms that make speech articulate and communicative. Like amphetamine it subjects people to a delusion of threat. This makes people violent, even murderous. Cocaine eventually contributed greatly to the unspeakable violence of ghetto life in the Eighties and Nineties.

Lysergic Acid is immediately hallucinatory. High claims have been made for it as access to the face of God. When hallucinations are as vivid in the perceptions as the real, reality is devalued and remains so after the drug has worn off. It also assists Structuralism insofar as it sees each human practice as belonging utterly to its genre, minimising or even cancelling the unique qualities of unfolding events. All fucks are just a fuck. All novels are just a novel. All arrive by process rather than praxis and are greeted with the kind of benign acknowledgement usually reserved for evening stars, rainbows and cuckoos. Post-modern irony is automatic.

Barbiturates make people sleepy, sloppy and incontinent.

Heroin bestows a sense of colossal health and well-being upon people who, because of an unfounded confidence induced by the drug, have drifted into poverty, debt, ill-health, restricted mobility and total corruptibility.

Drugs had no high profile in popular music until the artists moved in. A commonplace among French and American poets, Breton, Artaud, Cocteau, Ginsberg, Burroughs and the jazz musicians they revered, drugs came into Rock and Roll with art and, because they suddenly fused with the mass marketing machinery, extending their field of presence grossly. Rock and Roll was, by 1970, a cultural package deal that encapsulated the following:

a) A simplistic conservative musical form that substituted technological effects for creative development, but which was lively enough, accessible enough, aggressive enough and loud enough to keep everybody amused from the brilliant-but-bemused to the just-plain-thick.

b) An access to repetitive dress styles, each one originating in spontaneous youth rebellion, each one banked, marketed and recycled as rebellion diminished.

c) The delusion of genius in entertainers of modest talents and skills.

d) The delusion of historical and political consequence in the shuffling of styles, the belief that fashion-statements were social or political statements, the importance of this belief over and above any musical assessment of the work on stage.

e) The licence to transgress previous social and sexual taboos by public fornication, masturbation, homosexuality, vomiting, micturation, defecation and the scrapping of monogamy.

f) The use of illegal drugs and the pursuit of artificially altered awareness.

g) The substitution of image and spectacle for content and thought, of sensation for aesthetics, of a quality called 'attitude' demanded without anybody ever asking 'Which attitude?'

By 1970 the bid for saving the world had failed as the occupiers of universities and factories proved unable to set up administrative structures, proved unable to stand up to army guns and police batons, failed to persuade the working class, the trade unions, and the various Marxist organisations that the world needed saving by cultural transformation at great speed.

By 1970 Rock and Roll, the intermediary tool of transformation, had become the universal culture for all those under thirty. It was no longer the weapon of revolutionary artists. It was no longer a music of minority dissent. It dominated the streets, the clubs, the supermarkets, the shopping malls, radio and television. As young executives poured out of the revolutionary campuses into positions of control they paradoxically shared the culture that street addicts and militant outlaws still believed uniquely their own. Society dwelt under an impregnable dome of Rock and Roll. Under its shadow all elements of its package deal were not only accessible but expected. The access to the ignition of real change and progress was cut off. That which had been intended as a means to liberation, peace, love and truly humane inheritance for the species became, in the surviving hands of its entrepreneurial teams, a condition of control, stasis, decay and regression. Punk was rock lacerating itself in 1975, as it saw integrity slipping out of reach. This is the precise subject of the Sex Pistol's film *The Great Rock and Roll Swindle*.

3. EASY ALTERNATIVES

> Politics? I'm not sure that word means much any more.
> We probably need to invent a new word.
>
> > Sadie Plant, cyberfeminist.

Those under the Rock and Roll Dome saw themselves as separate from those outside it; indifferent, dismissive of all that had come before it; ignorant and disinterested in anything of a previous culture, for instance the agriculture of North Vietnam or the sexual brutality of Islam or the creative superiority of jazz. Initially, as the hipsters, the poets and the gurus fed them their palliative emergency ban-the-bomb mind-explosives, they were licensed by the absolute faith that they were a new consciousness that was going to defuse the old historic ballast that was locked in nuclear confrontation.

Under the Rock and Roll Dome the soft aspect of revolutionary consciousness was quickly seized. We may have failed to achieve nuclear disarmament, world government, world peace, but our failure didn't mean we had to go back to difficulty. A toke on a joint, an armful of skag and we were members of that special wisdom we fondly believed to be comparable to that of Buddhist and Hindu mystics, but Buddhism and Hinduism were outside the Dome so we had no way of verifying this piece of self-flattery.

In an immensely sweeping way the whole of history, even recent history, was lost into a soup of lazy generalisations. The two world wars were indistinguishable from one another and easily merged with the Boer War. Art Nouveau and Art Deco were interchangeable terms. Henry Mancini was a classical composer.

In the Dome's videotapes and films, period dress could be jumbled across centuries. The ancient debates of philosophy, politics, ethics and theology were all suddenly united as identical elements in old people's games. For Julie Burchill, jazz was a lot of old men in crumpled suits. For the pop group Queen, it needed no explanation to move from Bohemia, with a lightly sketched-in gypsy touch, to Renaissance Italy where Scaramouche could be lifted out of the ranks of the Comedia Del Arte, then immediately on to the more familiar territory of the American Midwest where some po' boy laments to his Mama that he done killed a man, all in one Rhapsody. The painful thorny creativity and political desperation that had promoted Rock and Roll so high above its previous status as fodder for sulky kids was now a joke among those same sulky kids. They had been given illusions of visionary superiority by chemicals that provoked an unsupported exultation as they ignited energies that were not implemented by stamina, intelligence or skill.

The certainty of the high was impenetrable. All who pointed out that the music, when you got past the glitter and the din, was nursery stuff, that society was depreciating rather than improving, and that the world was continuing its self-destructive course unimpeded, were simply not sharing the high, so lacked the one piece of awareness that enabled us to dismiss all the difficulties of the ages as self-perpetuating and tedious.

We had been told that our youth bestowed upon us an undeceived insight into the suicidal nature of history. We might not be able to do anything about that but at least we were licensed to refuse all difficulty. Instead of being healers we chose merely to be absolved of blame.

All advanced work in metaphysics, harmony, construction, social organisation, economic organisation and the wrenching paradoxes of good and evil, could be safely shirked. Sloth and hedonism enjoyed an open highway of rationalised permission. There might be a problem that we ourselves would get old and be as culpable as our parents under our own canon, but none of us believed that. Either we would die in nuclear holocaust or burn ourselves out like fireflies in the glorious brief incandescence of our chemical transport.

Now, as the Dome gets older and dowdier, many of us have no vocabulary for old age. Unable to move into the role of the quiet pipe and the prattle of grandchildren round the corner rocker, we pump HRT, testosterone and Viagra into our systems, we pursue diet, exercise, suntan and hairdye with the desperation of a horde of people losing identity. 'Seventy five years young,' we cry and some of us are persuaded that death has always anyway been part of the tedious backlog that the straights invented before Elvis. With the proper food, state of mind and the occasional transplant we can live as long as we want.

With the world of parents, grandparents and the illustrious dead so horrendous to us we must needs find alternatives and, indeed, 'alternative' became one of our favourite terms. In the world of alternative medicine, psychotherapy, agriculture, technology, cuisine, appointments were made without the tedious decisive knowledge-tests of the world before Elvis. Committees and examination boards, syllabi and mandatory data that had previously been necessary for professional practice were all deliriously irrelevant as we applied the inane certainties that flooded our veins to matters of life and death.

We made some headway where established practices were clogged with exploitation but we were not really able to take advantage of the wisdom of other cultures because we were sealed in our own where all our much vaunted primitivism could be betrayed by a glance at the video and the sound deck in the corner of the otherwise unfurnished room. We tended first to keep the villain of Western orthodoxy away from almost any other ethnic group whether we knew anything about them or not. Enfibulation, child marriage, slavery, crack-cocaine and a loose way of handling a machete could never compare with the widely known destructiveness of Jesus Christ, Beethoven, Shakespeare, Michelangelo, Pasteur, Curie, or even the British National Health System, the Welfare State and any democratic government. Only in surgery did we recognise a very real need for informed skills and treatments not open to interpretation. There is that about cutting and sewing up flesh that seems impervious to cultural conditioning. Once it becomes necessary the alternative possibility closes its forum. The waiter may become a poet or a priest, a psychiatrist or even a policeman, but we think differently when he picks up a scalpel.

Nonetheless, we were brave. In childbirth, the treatment of infected cuts, the treatment of schizophrenics and even sometimes the treatment of anything where straight medicine had failed, there was no harm in a spot of mollifying mumbo jumbo. Merrily we turned to homeopathy, tai-chi, yogi, acupuncture, physiotherapy, carrot cake and the munching of afterbirth, always staying in the shallow end of any beliefs that entailed challenging depths.

4.   DUMBING DOWN THE LAW

Britain 1995.
A grey-haired Irish woman sits on a comfortable sofa in her home in Manchester and talks about her son.

Her son is a lead singer in a new pop group that is notable for its similarity to the Beatles of thirty years ago.

'He's not a bad boy,' she says. 'High spirited you know. Always likes to cause a bit of devilment. Anything he says should be taken with, you know, a pinch of salt.'

Salt, the boy has implied in a newspaper interview, is by no means all that gets sniffed or pinched. Anxious to underline his street cred which is already strong he describes his childhood as a car thief and a vandal. Now he is surprised to find himself subject to a police inquiry. Who, for Christ's sake, do these bizzies think they are?

Law was an element of the world-before-Elvis for which we had a Dome-wide disregard. The same was true of family life as it has heretofore been known in North America and Western Europe.

Law was obviously difficult to accept because our impenetrable consensual wisdom was based on taking illegal chemicals. Everybody, even people who would tut-tut about TV licences and fare dodging, would cheerfully grow their plant or make their deal. The Dome existed outside the law. Increasingly stars were impervious to it. We implemented it when we wanted to jail brutal or incestuous fathers, reinstate sacked women or curtail the powers of the Drug Squad. On the other hand we would sometimes riot if there was any serious attempt to implement the law against drugs. We certainly believed that women had the right to condemn and execute their husbands and that black people had the right to do almost anything vengeful in the view of past abuses. All black politicians felt duty bound to declare all black defendants falsely accused. The trials of O.J. Simpson and Winston Silcott had to be conducted under threats of ghetto riot.

The heterosexual white male, on the other hand, had almost no rights. If the law would not punish him, alternative psychotherapy would. Self-trained, self-qualified consultants offered therapy modelled, more or less, on the twelve-step system pioneered by Alcoholics Anonymous. In order to test the ease of qualification, the comedian Bernard Manning applied and was accepted. By this system, with a little help from hypnosis and a reading in which Ellen Bass, Laura Davis, Alice Miller, Catherine McKinnon, and Andrea Dworkin replaced Freud, Adler, Jung, Winnicot and Klein, almost any act of heterosexual man could be interpreted and condemned as abuse.

And gradually, although art and politics had contributed so richly to setting up the Rock and Roll Dome, art and politics had been going on since year dot. Three chords and massive loudspeakers had thrust art into obscurity for the time being. And an alternative politics had to be found. If we declared women to be an oppressed class, and if we regarded all ethnic groups other than the European as unquestionably oppressed, we had the basis for Political Correctness which allowed us to shelve the patriarch Marx and the taxman Keynes, both of whom it was safe to equate with the old, white, heterosexual Hitler, even if you never said so.

The soil in which Political Correctness was planted was the American University Campus of the Seventies. Here is where it grew its most virulent crops. It was from here that graduates moved to establish the articles of Political Correctness through their new administrative roles in the media.

Each year universities are thronged with a fresh crop of frightened young men and women. Each year through the Seventies and the Eighties they became more frightened. Previously the only frightened ones were the ones that came from cloistered circumstances, convent schools or repressive homes in which the way of life was determined perhaps by a life-denying religion, or by devitalised elderly parents. The others couldn't wait to get at one another in those days. But increasingly the frightened ones were the children of the Rock and Roll Dome, brought up in a progressive privacy maintained by families frightened back to suburban isolation by drug use, paranoia and the need to stay home in cities where violence was running wild, a consequence of drug use at a lower class-level. They had been denied the normal rituals of pubertal courtship and coupling, yet they had been bombarded with a barrage of media-information in which orgasm and everybody's mandatory right to it was writ large. They were the children of separated, polygamous parents. The boys responded to their fear of girls by a boastful competitive assault, later converted to a masochistic apologetic grovelling. The girls responded to their fear of the boys by backing into the defensive groups so readily provided by Feminism, in Women's Centres and Rape Crisis Centres now mandatory on campuses where Women's Studies and Gender Studies thrived as legitimate disciplines. Both boys and girls, besides being scared of one another, were scared of strangers and scared of sex in general, not confusing it in any way with love, in fact by this time not using the l-word much.

Here they were compensated in their terror by being given guidelines of behaviour in which women were declared to be victimised in all their possible relationships with men. Leering, smiling, winking, waving and whistling were all condemned as exploitative and redefined as harassment. The fear was not healed. It was condoned and underpinned. It was directed into sublimatory programmes of protest, reclaiming nights and stringing blue alarm lights everywhere. Intercourse was only to be consented to by signature. The tenderest or most cautious caress, or even a comforting embrace, were interpreted as violence. In the contemporary muddying of truth such inverted interpretation can become widespread without difficulty.

Catherine McKinnon was a main mover here, conducting a crusade from campus to campus, whipping up hysteria seldom seen since the McCarthy trials, exploiting fear and condemning love and heterosexual coupling, the fundamental pivots of human life.

The intense and transcendental passion which sexual lovers have for one another, the two way exchange of dominion and obeisance they achieve, the inspiration of poetry and music out of which a humane free society has at least been attempted in the West, was utterly destroyed. In a climate so created it became inevitable that a young and otherwise admirable headmistress should refuse to send her pupils to a performance of *Romeo and Juliet*.

Political Correctness addressed itself to words, changing meaning so radically as to almost annul meaning completely. A lexicon of euphemisms was coined. Disability had curiously come to be regarded as a cause for shame and embarrassment so, like a skeleton in the family cupboard or a paedophilic relative, must never be mentioned by its plain names. Disabled people were not disabled; they were 'exceptional.' Deaf people were 'aurally challenged.' Retarded people were 'mentally challenged.' Blind people were 'optically challenged.' Psychotics were 'socially misaligned.' Aspects of normality also became unmentionables. Male heterosexuality was 'testosterone poisoning.' Prostitutes were 'sex care providers.' Crooks were 'morally different.' The odours of the body were 'non-discretionary fragrance.' To be pissed or stoned was to be 'chemically inconvenienced.' Stockbreeding and poultry-breeding were 'anthropocentrism.' The recognition of Europe's leading role in civilisation was 'boreocentrism.' Terms differentiating between the sexes, man and woman for instance, were rigorously if somewhat hopelessly attacked. Because the initiators of these linguistic cleansings had been too intensely dedicated to the crusade they actually hadn't done much work on their word-roots, you got 'personagement committee,' 'personual control,' and 'femstruation.'

The aim was the imposition of a naively simplistic egalitarianism in which animals and plants enjoyed equal rights with all human individuals and heterosexual Caucasian males were seen as inevitable oppressors and predators, particularly if they were telling the truth. The casualties were the structures of society, all society, and nature whose vital predatory and reproductive systems were ignored, as were the inconvenient survival of slavery in liberated African states, the total oppression of women under Islam and the termination of slavery in Europe and North America. Close examination quickly revealed that the model of relationships which Political Correctness held to be universal was the middle-class suburb where, indeed, businessman fathers called the tune, Mom was condemned to a hostess role, everyone gathered round for the hypermarketed, battery-reared Sunday roast, the gardens were sprinkled with pesticide and weed-killer, blacks, Latins, and homosexuals were only welcomed with unease, and the basic shape of civilisation was laid out alphabetically by the Encyclopaedia in the lounge book-case. This was precisely the environment from which citizens of the Dome had originally dropped out, against which they felt they should fabricate their alternative political programmes, granted rebellion by the music and insight by drugs.

The initiators of Political Correctness had suffered little contact with the working class, now retitled the underclass. Class was a pre-Elvis irrelevancy and nobody any longer need soil their rock credibility by being seen with anyone in a pit helmet or with their hair in curlers. This was more urgent in America where the working class had been right-wing for years. That redneck racialism was the consequence of cultural starvation had been explained too long ago to carry weight under the Dome.

Obscure figures like Reich, Gurdjieff and Ouspenski loomed into acceptability early on even though some of them had contributed to the formative development of patriarchs like Hitler, Stalin and D.H. Lawrence.

5. INNER REALITY

The Rock and Roll Dome, like a cathedral, a mosque or any edifice of consensual, unchallenged, irrational conviction, is a dream and all within it have exchanged the dream for reality.

Marijuana, heroin and the barbiturates have a wonderful way of disconnecting our natural alarm systems whereby we sense urgency in providing for ourselves and our loved ones, whereby we ward off danger.

Part of the original humanitarian revolutionary intent was to break through the restrictive conditioning of society whereby crown, church, state, family and neighbourhood had debased life for centuries. Indeed great groundwork was done in challenging the vengeful hand of God following transgression of sexual and social codes. We wore denims to the Commemoration Ball and fucked each other in the face and the arse and nothing came out of the clouds to strike us dead. Sadly, in doing so we blinded ourselves to the addictive properties of our means, to the viciousness of the untempered libido in either sex, and to the uncontrollable viciousness of capitalism. Sleeping in cardboard boxes, soliciting on the Bradford streets with a black eye, buying Japanese shares in the Year of the Earthquake, correcting Balkan dictators, we still cry 'Paranoia!' when anybody says 'Careful!'

The amphetamines and cocaine had a wonderful way of bestowing upon us all a sense of god-like power, something long-hungered for in a society that had thrown up such dream models as Superman and Wonder Woman. The more literate were able to connect Clark Kent with Nietzsche. It was only the narrow switched-off world before Elvis that had fobbed us off with lies about our inability to fly and strike down evil by remote control.

The hallucinogenics like lysergic acid, mescaline and mushrooms so mingled received experiences with projected experiences that it was easy to cheerfully sacrifice the ability to distinguish between the two.

'Fascism' became the ready term for any discord in the equanimity of our dream. 'Paranoic fascism' had, up until Elvis, deceived us into thinking that the outer world was real and the inner world was not. The reality of dream was impeded by the false finality of the reality bestowed upon the external world.

Our dream, a human right that had been stolen long ago, had been reclaimed by means of these wondrous liquids and powders commonly used by the shamans of uncontaminated cultures from Dawson City to Llasa. This was the importance of Dr Timothy Leary's oft-quoted slogan 'Turn on. Tune in. Drop out.' We turned on to the common binding ecstasy of being human on the planet. We turned on to the inner light and the inner space with considerable sublimating rationale from Carlos Casteeda and R.D. Laing. We tuned in to the great collective mind of humanity.

And we dropped out into the Rock and Roll Dome. The trouble was that when we got our breath in the late seventies we discovered that the media, the stock-exchange, the white-collar classes and the American Army in Vietnam had dropped out with us.

To the entire turned-on scene, in which the starchy pinstripe disguise of barristers and cabinet ministers had become entirely transparent, fact, the indication of fact, the awareness of fact and persistent presence of fact in nature and mortality, was enemy material. We directed our thinking towards the rationalisation of dissolving, clouding, disregarding, or, if possible, disproving fact, although proof was part of the vocabulary of pre-Elvis thinking that believed in facts anyway. Facts were, we said, the coinage of factualism and the Structuralists agreed with us that factualism was a belief-system. Facts were often claimed as the basis for paranoid fascism. It was in the pre-Elvis world that we believed we came into the world by copulation and gestation, that we left the world by death, and that we fed our social structure by predatory material disciplines such as mining and agriculture as certainly as birds fed on insects and wolves fed on lambs. Paranoid fascists like Galileo and Newton believed this to be original and final. A condition.

The family then, as a necessary unit, must be the first to go. Family, already condemned by Laing, Esterson and Cooper as the crucible of psychosis, was the primal patriarchy, the very origin of dictatorship. Fathers were fathers not because of their participation in the necessity of reproduction, a process which, despite sore hardship, was still seen as somehow wonderful up until Elvis. Fathers were fathers because they were strong, male and brutal. Instead of inheriting a function they had created a role in order to exercise power. It was widely preached, from the otherwise intelligent Germaine Greer to the dangerously rabid McKinnon and Dworkin, that testosterone made monsters out of half the human race, the half with pricks, and that the urge to fuck was the urge to stab. This glib equation was clearly only possible amongst those who had been spared the rigours both of maintaining an erection and of bayonet training, who were consequently bound to be unaware of the difference between disobedient gristle and tempered steel.

Following this relegation of natural fact from the status of axiom to the status of arguable, and therefore alterable, notion, it was a short step to believe sex itself to be an idea, an aspiration, not a condition of the inherited flesh but an aspiration of inner space, a part of the self which, because central, was held to be more authentic than appearance or form. Who cares about cocks and cunts, testes and ovaries, when the true self must be given a choice. We pinched the word 'gender' from linguistics where it was used in the sub-division of nouns in the grammar of the romance languages, and started to use it instead of the term 'sex'. We derailed biological fact out of the biological area into the area of dream where we could do what we liked with it. Nobody so far has got any comic footage out of the fact that the wish to change gender might be a man's wish to be a table or any other feminine object; the fact that *con* (cunt in French) is masculine offers some opportunity for humour.

Thus, conveniently, we achieved what we had wanted to do for some time. We wrested sex from reproduction and started to talk about it as though it had never had that function or that condition.

The Rock and Roll dream welcomed the Structuralist contention of the world as mind and Structuralist philosophers facilitated the dreamers' wish to avoid dilemma. Thus the awful finality of assessible quality could be ditched. Excellence and creative success ceased to be impediments to the creative rights of all strummers, doodlers and crack-brained pundits in the university of life. Those who pointed out that compositional assets in the Beatles' music were, although delightful, a long way short of those demanded by the Fab Four's god-like status, could be dismissed as peers enjoying a notion of quality to which they had a perfect right but which was, nonetheless, a notion, no better than the notion of those who openly set Lennon and McCartney alongside Schubert and Mozart. Mediocrity was licensed by this ambivalent egalitarianism. Not only were those unfortunate in sensitivity, even to the extent of tone-deafness, colour blindness or dyslexia, welcomed to contribute to the work, but a fiction of tribalism was attempted in the decoration of body and clothing, in the skirling of recorders and the rattling of bongo drums, which had no codes, no rituals, no formulae to test and ratify the contribution to the ceremony. Theatre groups and communes expressed themselves joyously together believing themselves to be in no way inferior to ceilidh bands or chapel choirs because their notion of merit had a human right to equality with any other. Beneath the egalitarianism was the effervescent hubris of those who were switched on (i.e. drugged) as against those who floundered with the prehistoric. The universities where excellence must be advertised to attain status while any were accepted to fill courses and reap fees, loomed into view.

The floodgates were also open for the assertion that the art of undeveloped societies was to be held on an equal standing with that of epoch-making masterwork. Fry and Bell set African carving alongside Michelangelo. Cubists and Surrealists delighted in the esoteric, but had no focus on the fact that it was the Cubist and Surrealist delight that had historic potency rather than tribal art that hadn't changed a lot since the Stone Age. Then came Political Correctness with its uninformed hunger for the ethnic and its dismissal in particular of Dead White European Males. The obvious fact that a fair number of the Dead White European Paranoic Fascists were predominantly Latin or Semitic, and a significant minority were women, was one of many flaws in the simplistic fabric of the universal pseudo-political creed.

In the study of art, criticism of the work of young artists by experienced artists or by perceptive critics like Walter Benjamin, Bronowski, Berger or Heron, receded into disrepute if not ridicule. These pedants with their untenable outdated certainties of assessment could be humoured until silent. Forward came the art historians and sociologists who, instead of recognising achievement by pleasure in that achievement, and displeasure in failure, allocated all work equal importance as evidence of the societal structure of its time.

Thus concerts, exhibitions and books ceased to be focal points of excitement from which the human spirit could be rekindled and redirected, and became instead museums of the present in which all evidence was as illustrative of society's flavour as it had ever been.

Under such a critical canon, the poignancy of a Woodbine packet served as well as that of a Paul Nash painting. Both were part of British culture in the early twentieth Century. Art was robbed of its culturally stimulating function and ephemera were promoted to the same value as art. Bogart's trilby was worth as much as Chandler's prose.

Burroughs' paintings, colour enhanced pistol targets, were worth as much as the revolutionary syntax and the mordant satire of his prose, despite the way it fed the movie techniques of Peckinpah, Godard and Roeg. Moving easily on runners provided by the Dada and Surrealist use of found objects, artists' products became little more than the ephemera of their lives. In fact in the Nineties, Tracey Emin opened a gallery to continually exhibit the ephemera of her life, stained garments, electric bills, anything at all presented in such a way as to suggest that a life of trivial and sordid misadventure is in some way evidence of the martyrdom of women.

The densely thronged 1996 Cézanne exhibition, when finally shown in Britain outside its proud mother country, was received with a desperate journalistic barrage to read it as evidence of his relationship with Flaubert, as misogyny towards the adored Mme Cézanne, as Nineteenth Century sentimental ruralism, as a coding of sexual imagery, as the start of Provençal tourism, indeed as anything except the magnificent display of the way planes resonate and collide dynamically in light and space, to provide a new and different spatial pleasure from that of receding horizons and chiaroscuro volume. The facts thus revealed and celebrated, and the fact of Cézanne's skill in making them manifest, had become invisible to every single commentator whose job it was to elucidate upon the subject.

Why then the throngs? Was there a profound hunger beginning to be felt? Were people of the Rock and Roll Dome beginning to feel the lack of something taken away from them?

Leeds. 1976.
From my morning perch at the turn of the balcony stairs overlooking the main Fine Art studio I can see Simon Gartside make his entrance.

Gartside had been at Leeds over a year and has done barely enough work to validate his presence. Nonetheless he carries himself in no distress, or even any concern, about his serious creative constipation. While other students suffer an early block through insecurity, culture shock, or just plain dope, Simon Gartside's paralysis seems to be brought on by his own contempt for the Department. A tall beautiful young man with long hippie hair, immaculately groomed to a subtle golden brown, his demeanour is poised elegantly in lassitude and a short of disappointed dignity. He disappears for long periods to Wales where pals from his foundation course with whom he had a band are settled preparing music and strategy for fun to come.

Simon came to Leeds on wings of expectation. Brian Eno had been around, never a student, but living with a student and eavesdropping on the dialogue. Tony Scott who distinguished himself by precipitating public copulation in his foam bath at the Isle of Wight Rock Festival was around in a similar capacity. The author of **Bomb Culture** *(myself) was on the staff. The policy was wide-open liberty with all facilities of space, materials and machinery available to all students whose imagination was permitted to extend its range to film, performance, writing and tape composition, beyond the usual painting and sculpture. All you needed to be, at Leeds in the Seventies, was diverse. All that was forbidden was the dull. The* course was a kind of concert platform where sooner or later you had to do your turn. All this made Leeds Fine Art well known and promised three years spent in the teeth of advancement. What was frequently daunting to students from the south was the predominance of working class kids from northern industrial cities, the so-called woollybacks, with more interest in Tetley's bitter than in clothes and transcendental drugs. There seemed little concern for the importance of the content of fashion and a rather tedious, out-dated belief in idiosyncrasy.

Each day Simon attended, splendid in near-feminine robes and colours, with careful eyeshadow and a little rouge indicating his awareness that Roxy Music and David Bowie were, between them, transcending the old romanticism of the Stones and Pink Floyd. Unwilling to abandon the style which his pals in Wales still espoused, he used his girlfriend to thoroughly observe the new direction. She wore formal male, charcoal grey suit, white shirt and tie, and wore her hair in a Bertie Wooster crop, heavily larded and combed back. Arm in arm and unsmiling, they made a considered, self-conscious fashion statement which I sometimes thought was supposed to be assessed as their work.

A year later Simon Gartside has broken with his hippie mates in Wales and is planning a band with Sebastian Morley which will be called Scritti Politi. Simon will become Green and Sebastian will become Tom Soviet. The extraordinary semantics of this piece of Communist campery owes at least something to the vague Marxism of the Art Language Fine Art Course at the nearby university which Simon, in a flounce of annoyance at being ignored by the Polytechnic students and staff, has unofficially joined. Here he's given the flattering multi-syllabic polemic with which to flog the flyblown Nineteenth Century individualism he was unable to join.

While the Fine Art staff are marking his year for degrees, Simon contributes to the degree show by taking a series of photographs of staff, biros in hand, spiral notebooks poised, deciding on the numerical worth of students' efforts.

He does this in blithe and perilous ridicule. Once departed, having refused a degree which he wasn't going to get anyway, he publishes an account of his course at Leeds in Studio International. Most of it has had to be blocked out so that the whole article looks like an oddly shaped crossword puzzle.

As Gartside is smiling his supercilious smirk and snapping his camera, Marc Almond and David Ball are in the Department's sound studio making their first tape.

6. PERSONAL SPACES

> The acquisition of my tape recorder really finished
> whatever emotional life I might have had, but I was
> glad to see it go – I think that once you see emotions
> from a certain angle you can never think of them as
> real again. That's more or less what happened to me.
>
> Andy Warhol

Rochdale and London 1984

It is some months now since I gave up at Liverpool. I attempted to translate the free field of individual imaginative exploration, that proved so successful at Leeds over the decades, to Liverpool with its separate 'healthy' rivalry between the Sculpture Department and the Painting Department, with its faith in competitive cadres loyal to their manual skills. I failed. Starved of money by a bureaucracy of technophiles who believed Fine Art to be as redundant as alchemy and dowsing, alienated from my own staff by my insistence on politicised personal vision, I find myself early retired, teaching life-drawing one day a week at Rochdale.

The life studio, a one-time weaving loft, looks out over the rainy slates of the semi-derelict mill-town. I lean on the windowsill dreaming of lost ladies while the students beaver away with their pencils, brushes and sticks of charcoal.

Compelled to use two models because two are contracted, I decide to make a virtue of necessity and intertwine them. They are back to back with elbows interlocked on one side and vertical arms interlocked at the wrist on the other. I have asked them if the pose will be easier to hold if I join their wrists with paper masking tape. That would help they say, so I do it.

The phone jangles in the office. 'A call for you Mr. Nuttall,' says the secretary who is in the main building two streets away. It is Toby, one of my five sons.

'It's Tim,' he says. 'I can't handle him. I need help.'

Toby and Tim were the real musical talent among my kids, Toby a guitarist in the classic blues-based mode of the rock soloists, Tim a drummer capable of rare dynamic complexities. Tim has a problem — the enormity of his dream, his total immersion in it, has barely contained messianic aspirations. I have already helped to cure Tim of heroin use by shopping his dealer. Now, Toby tells me with some desperation, he has turned to amphetamine sulphate and is pursued by a Satanic execution squad of spidermen.

They are surrounding Toby's flat where Tim is dithering and weeping in abject terror. A doctor has seen him and has prescribed total detox, even from caffeine and tobacco. The spidermen, however, are still there.

I am distressed by this news. Tim is a son with whom I have been very close. Shedding the smack was not exactly a holiday and now the angel's wings have burnt again, dropping him back in the sewer of real paranoia.

The models and the students look happy for the time being. I nip next door to the pub for a swift double. When I return the studio is empty.

The head of the course tells me he is going to have to sack me. Feminists among the students have convinced the models that I have tricked them into a bondage pose and have persuaded them to protest. The head, an old friend and one-time colleague of Stuart Brisley, sacks me. The next day I take a train to London to collect Tim.

The flat is halfway up a long hill in Camden Town. It is easily discernible from the taxi because the door is ineptly daubed with cabalistic insignia in cheap gloss primaries. The household of musicians, performance artists and just plain dopers, is grouped about in moving but inadequate concern for Tim who sits in their midst smiling at the ludicrousness and the inevitability of my arrival and the need for it.

Toby fills me in while Tim giggles. His face, as usual, is grey with London grime, punctuated with zits and an uneven growth of ginger fuzz. He rolls a straight with toffee-coloured fingers, sets it in a mouth where teeth of the same colour can be glimpsed and lights it. Then he realises that I'm going to take him out where the spidermen are waiting and so bursts into tears, ruining his cigarette with saliva and throws a cup of tea at me. He misses, hits the wall where the tea dregs it contained trickle slowly to the floor. I embrace him until the spasm has passed.

I go and get a taxi, cuddle him into it and get him to Kings Cross where the police are out in armed splendour to protect us from expected football supporters. Getting Tim through this incipient battleground is like getting a phobic through a snake pit.

Once on the train his mood transforms. His intelligence is still there and can be nourished with truth and humour.

Under the sealed Dome of Rock and Roll everyone believed themselves to be united. Discussion, debate, contests in reason and persuasion, comparison of data, was, at a stroke, declared irrelevant. As its substitute there was a new ceremony called consciousness-raising in which hordes of people discovered, or at least pretended, they agreed. This ranged from clusters around the gurus like the Maharishi in the Sixties and the Bagwan in the Eighties, through hysterical sessions of the early Seventies in which women who had been visible to one another all their lives, somehow, in a different sense, 'found one another' in the declaration of common, previously secret, needs; on to the confessional orgies precipitated by Catherine McKinnon and Andrea Dworkin on American campuses. At all Rock and Roll performances, many of which were on a Billy Graham scale, seating was removed so that the audience could stand in their fervent salutation of their star, hands raised, voices chorusing in a unison identical to that of the Nazi gatherings. The almost endearing flinging of cum-sodden knickers that had characterised the Fifties rock performances was left far behind.

From the first toke the smoker was 'tuned in' not just to others at the gathering but to a whole generation, a world-wide homogenous consciousness. At parties people who had previously embraced, swapped jokes, hived off for flirtation and sex, for political argument, for heartfelt talk, just embraced, then moved off to their corner where, under the waves of sound so loud it prevented conversation, even were it required, they took their drug and communicated by merely relaxing into a shared state of belonging.

This shared state was the saddest delusion of all those delusions of the Rock and Roll dream. The belief that a delusion is as good as a perception didn't prevent them drifting in separate directions as soon as their wordlessness prevailed. Along those private courses (which were, inevitably, ignorant of the direction other dreamers had taken) fear and distrust quickly set in, which, because they had set into minds inflamed by debilitating chemicals, swiftly developed into paranoia. Accounts of plots, poisoning, giro thefts, infidelities, evil spells and secret world domination organisations all became the commonplaces of the communes and squats, even generating some of the best fiction of the Rock and Roll dream – books like Richard Farina's *Been Down So Long It Looks Like Up To Me*, Thomas Pynchon's *Gravity's Rainbow* and *V*. Conspiracy theories seethed in all William Burroughs' writing.

With delusion of unity under this sealed dome which no healing sense could penetrate, a separation of each individual began to manifest itself.

Popular dance had been a ceremony of pairing for 100 years, from the Waltz and the Polka to the belly to belly embraces of the Mecca and the Locarno dance halls. With rock things changed. The flinging of one another about in the old Fifties Rock and Roll dance, a violent mutual coupling, then gave way to the Twist.

In the Twist the couple remained but had lost touch. They gyrated opposite one another grinding and bumping their genital regions in a monotonous trance that was never to be tested, resolved or terminated. It was the sexual, musical equivalent of staying high, of not coming down; the unchanging perpetuations of drug-use had been substituted for the sequence of climactic acts as the number and the tempi changed in previous dancing.

Then, when acid arrived, the couples split up completely. Each dancer occupied an isolated space, eyes closed, inwardly focused, often dancing whether there was music or not. Musicians were similarly separated, their previous empathy on the stand replaced by a sound technician. This was the way we danced when walkmans arrived in the Seventies, ensuring that we not only were released from a partner and a shared space, but that we also each enjoyed separate music, audible only to the one with the earphones. By the late Eighties the music was machine-made repetition. People isolated by Ecstasy and hysteria, danced to exhaustion and sometimes to death.

Insofar as music and dance are voluptuous arts traditionally connected with coupling, and insofar as Rock and Roll dancing was a development of the overt sexuality of jazz dancing, the Rock and Roll culture had moved into a new sexuality.

Rock and Roll paranoia had exchanged intercourse, with its pleasure in the giving of pleasure, with its voluptuous homage to the other, with its telling and enhancing tributaries into caring and reproduction, indeed with its measures of pantheism and unity with nature that were so prominent a part of the Rock and Roll dream of the Sixties, for masturbation. My pleasure, we each one of us said, is mine, just as surely as my stash is mine. It is not generated by you and has nothing to do with any feelings I may have for you. Rather than risk what my drug-paranoia has made me fear from you, I will retract into a reduced activity, one which carries no adventure, no revelation, no wonderment and certainly no love except the love I may feel for myself and my life. The love which, for a season was 'all we needed', lost its location. It ceased to be an exchange and became a private trance.

Thus, with sex genitally located, intercourse, when it took place, was almost preferable with strangers; it had lost the awesomeness that comes with its life-giving powers and had become a casual cruising, a use of one another rather than a deeply felt honouring of one another. We pursued and achieved orgasms and sometimes compared them like people comparing new purchases. A kiss, however, that was something else. The personal commitment embodied in a lover's kiss was felt to be more threatening than unwanted pregnancy and syphilis had once been. Kissing thinned in the social arena, despised as a softening and a sentimentalisation of the self-seeking sexuality which, by now, had become something of a personal career. Caring became, increasingly, not an emotion by which one was burdened but a social responsibility allocated to those being paid for it. Anyone else recoiled from it.

London

It is '68, the year after the year of love. The revolution is still rumbling on the streets of Paris. The art schools and the universities are still occupied. The whole thing was precipitated in this country by poets and poetry. The Albert Hall reading saw the butterfly of hippiedom emerge from the chrysalis of CND. The centres were still bookshops and poetry readings were still as important as rock concerts on the revolutionary cultural calendar. Mike Horovitz is running a reading in the bar of a London theatre. He is helped in this by a young and pleasant woman who is responsible for bar events.

Pete Brown has been drumming. The poems have come fast and furious — Ivor Cutler, Spike Hawkins, Mike, me, with a tidal wave of applause following each.

I am on a roll of success. **Bomb Culture** *has just come out to widespread rave reviews. My poems are in Penguin and I've escaped secondary modern schoolteaching to a job at Bradford Art School.*

I stagger off the stand, breaking through the applause like a swimmer, grab a bottle of Newcastle Brown, pour it, drink it and turn as the house-manager passes.

'Kiss me,' I say.

'No,' she says.

A promiscuity previously peculiar to homosexuals became, with the Rock and Roll culture, everybody's expectation of a mandatory sexual right, inflamed and promoted by a new wave of magazines such as *Cosmopolitan* and *Under 18*. Homosexuals escalated into unheard-of levels of promiscuity, developing a widespread addiction to orgasm as intense as any narcotic addiction, borrowing its psychological pattern from narcotic addiction itself and ultimately proving as destructive and degrading.

Under the Rock and Roll Dome we had long forgotten syphilis and gonorrhoea. Penicillin had been a convenience of life for us since, if not before Elvis, before the Beatles. We had also forgotten, or never known, unreliable birth control. We were astonished when AIDS arrived though anyone could have foreseen that such a violent acceleration in promiscuity was bound to have some medical consequence. The condom returned as an AIDS preventative about the time that feminists condemned the pill. Under the Rock and Roll Dome no-one remembered that the newly fashionable condom was about as reliable a method of birth control as school blotting paper. Also the necessity of flesh-to-flesh in mutual sex had been lost in our sexuality of self-pleasuring.

In the age in which facts were cancelled and ideas held to be the universal material of existence it was difficult for us to receive the fact of an epidemic disease. Time and again we veered off in attempts to read it as ideology. Some of us were convinced it was spread by the CIA to destroy the alternative society. Others declared it a consequence of African Satanism. It was, others insisted, a redneck plot against homosexuals. To declare that the obvious vulnerability of homosexuals to AIDS should be treated as a guide to its cause was held to be homophobic propaganda. This is partly the consequence of the way in which the whole epidemic was subject to political (and Politically Correct) hysteria from the start. Homosexuals involved in dealing with the crisis in the early stage concluded, in the midst of a persecution panic, that money would not be forthcoming from a staid and straight medical authority unless heterosexuals also felt threatened. The danger of heterosexuals contracting AIDS was always comparatively slight but, because AIDS publicity was in the hands of homosexuals who perpetuated the myth of heterosexual vulnerability in order to gain credibility and support, the heterosexual community was thrown into a panic that severely damaged heterosexual pleasure, while homosexuals were denied the priority they needed in warning-publicity and medical treatment. This continued until Jamie Taylor of Gay Men Fighting AIDS blew the gaff on Radio 4's *Today* programme. Information that the anus and the throat were more fragile than the vagina, thus rendering homosexuals more prone to the disease, was suppressed from national media publicity by Margaret Thatcher who found such information distasteful. To declare that promiscuity was its cause was held to be a fundamentalist Christian reading of AIDS.

Gay Men Fighting AIDS was one of the many rapidly formed support groups. The folded red ribbon appeared ostensibly to declare AIDS consciousness, whatever that may have ever been. Quickly, like the CND badge in the Fifties, it broadened its meaning. It become fashionable and, having proliferated on the shirt-fronts of the Rock and Roll world, it came to indicate a militancy in defence of the human right to a Politically Correct promiscuity that avoided dominant husbands. Jewellers cast AIDS ribbons in gold, while magazines, T-shirts, films and AIDS-conscious rock numbers that never mentioned cancer, meningitis or narcotic brain-damage, sold by the million under the strange phenomenon of a disease becoming a media topic of immense marketing power. That the ribbon was worn by many people who were simultaneously condemning the sexuality of all heterosexual males, even seeking to raise the female age of consent to twenty-one, thus prolonging the childhood of women by ten years, is one of the more richly ironic anomalies of the Rock and Roll Dome in full decay.

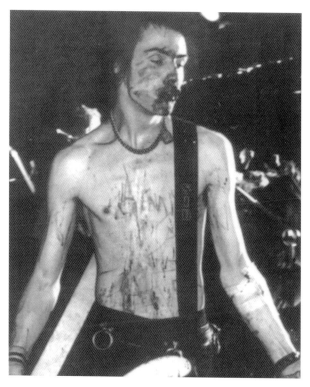

Sid Vicious.

Courtney Love.

The separation of individuals under the Rock and Roll Dome could conceivably be connected to the massively disguised suburban nature of Rock and Roll culture. Beyond all pretences to street credibility, beyond the lionisation of the delinquent, the punk, the motor-cycle nomad, the rhyzomatic, there was a middle-class romanticism of the social deviant. It was a militant rebellion against the repression of suburban respectability that sent these progeny of secure loving families off into the boozing of Janis Joplin, the self laceration of Kurt Cobain, Richie Edwards, Courtney Love and Sid Vicious, more than it was poverty, underprivilege or parental abuse.

It was natural, then, that as drugs effected isolation, so the drugs isolation of individuals welded with the old-fashioned privacy of the semi-detached villa, the closed front door, the opaque glass and the high privet hedge. A suburban ethic of mandatory privacy is clearly discernible in the extraordinary notion of personal space. In the United States this is intensified in the ethic of the security patrolled residential estate, fenced off from the very deviants that Rock and Roll romanticises and where so many millionaires of the Rock and Roll industry live. It was from such cloistered homes that the architects of Political Correctness came.

Richie Edwards.
... self laceration ...

London. 1986
We have a long and mildly boozy lunch in the Almeida Restaurant-Bar. She is a little off her patch, socially speaking. Dark, incandescent, sharp, simultaneously intolerant and sympathetic, she is an habituée of what remains of bohemian Soho now that Colquhoun, MacBride, Dylan, Muriel and Francis Bacon are all dead.

I ride her home in my rust-pocked old Volvo, Ellington pouring out of the loudspeakers. 'Great system,' she says. She doesn't say 'Hodges!' Nevertheless, lust is churning steadily somewhere just to the back of my iliac crest.

She lives in a comfortable, oddly grouped jumble of rooms that must once have been a shop. She is clearly uneasy about my presence in them. There is an edge in the atmosphere that tells me that if there's to be sex it won't be here this afternoon. I finish my whisky and she shows me out. A second before I say goodbye I kiss her and she receives my kiss. 'A kiss,' she says moodily 'is more intimate than a fuck.' Still holding her face in my hands I say: 'I intend intimacy. I'm after ya,' with a Yorkshire inflection that taints my voice whenever I want to be unambiguous. Then I walk towards the car.

'Fuck off!' she shrieks and, as I glance back, she is doubled like a poised viper in a coil of hatred, giving me the finger as though shafting my brain.

Personal space is an extraordinary notion, in no way less ridiculous than personal sunlight, personal drinking water, or personal rain. In effect it assumed a tacitly acknowledged albeit invisible privet hedge around each individual wherever they happened to be or to go. Along the way in which dwellers in large cities conducted themselves, avoiding eye-contact and ignoring the greetings of strangers, it laid claim to everybody's right to remain unapproachable until they chose to invite.

This was a swift recoil from the early belief in the Rock and Roll Dome that indiscriminate intimacy and touch was humanly healing, a necessary step to world peace. In the prevalence of sex-with-strangers the belief survived but there was an inversion of quality and significance between the Sixties love-in (the grope heap in British Arts Laboratories in which young people in various stages of undress entwined themselves into a collective knot of stimulation on a mattress in a dim-lit room, the anti-alienation touch-experience of theatre and performance art groups) and the rigidly formal codes of stop-go-stop that allow totally anonymous participants to use each other for pleasure in the contemporary sex club. The first was an attempt to surmount the ego, the second a determination to be independent.

Personal space is a strategy. Suburbanites found themselves in a culture whose initial crusade against alienation had placed them in a situation bereft of the privacy their upbringing had led them to believe to be as mandatory as education and legal protection. Quickly they retracted to the ethics of their homelands. Out came old notions of privacy. Working with drug paranoia and masturbatory sex, they served to isolate citizens of the Rock and Roll Dome, one from another, still further.

Feminists particularly were swift to grasp the new isolation. Stiff-jawed and sore-arsed from the orgy, they had already decided, many of them, that the sexually arrogant rock star, who bestowed the right to fellate him upon his adolescent fans as a priest bestowing favours on the poor of the parish, was representative of the entire male species. Every simple nuance of imaginative vengeful loathing was deployed to condemn, refuse, reject and destroy male sexuality. Radical feminists like Sheila Jeffreys advocated the removal of the male population of the world to arctic camps whence they would provide well-chilled sperm for a lesbian society. This programme was seriously discussed and even applauded. Organised cadres of feminists ranged the streets in industrial cities beating up men as blackshirts had once beat up Jews.

Glen Matlock with Fans, as a priest bestowing favours ...

Personal space, expressed in slogans and notions like *Our Lives Our Bodies, Their Hands On Our Bodies*, was a strong element in the asinine conventions established by McKinnon and Dworkin. Body-as-property took priority over body as the medium of love. Personal space intensified to generate such concepts as Date Rape, Sexual Harassment, Verbal Rape, Optical Rape. Each of these notions involved a condemnation of courtship. Courtship in all society had, of course, involved an essential exchange of initiatives and advances. Traditionally, as celebrated in song and dance from English folksong to the formalities of Japanese drama, courtship incorporates a good deal of yes-no-maybe on the part of whoever's being wooed, usually the woman. To deliver a clunking NO MEANS NO may have been necessary in situations where raging ego-maniacs of the Rock and Roll stage were scything through fans with their insatiable pricks out, but, repeated as a neurotic human rule, it ignored completely the frou-frou, the delicate to-and-fro of civilised courtship. The lost dance of delicious tension was, of course, lost because it belonged to the world before Elvis. No-one knew that for most of the history of humanity a sexuality in which No meant No was a pretty dull one.

No-one had noticed that, in all these puritanical drives we had lost all respect and all love for our own species. Wonderment and adoration were kept for the mirror. In our pursuit of freedom and equality we had emerged from the common tuned-in consciousness of Timothy Leary to render one another worthless.

Meanwhile the necessary word 'rape', having been applied to glances up skirts, saucy winks and wolf whistles, had lost its meaning, as the terrible depths of sexual brutality had lost all perspective on its evil when it was equated with the ordinary stirrings of boy-girl manoeuvres. Similarly the term 'harassment' lost meaning when it was applied to a single experimental gesture as much as to a repetitive persistent nuisance.

People wishing to be rescued from all sex except sex as an aid to masturbation were going to have similar problems with politics. The original politicisation of Rock and Roll having failed dismally in 1968, those of us who moved on to various forms of orthodox Marxism found commitment to collective needs a gross intrusion on 'doing our own thing in our own time.' There was not much point in releasing yourself from the stringencies of the work ethic by 'dropping out' only to embrace the more exacting stringencies of the party line. In any case reconciliation between dialectical materialism and the narcotic dream had proved impossible when André Breton attempted it and it remained impossible in the Seventies. Nuclear disarmers at Greenham Common practically forgot the nuclear rockets so preoccupied were they with excluding men.

How was a Rock and Roll Dome citizen, isolated by drugs, masturbatory sex and personal space, to maintain any political credentials whatsoever? Somehow the alternative must retain something of its crusading character. The answer came in ecology. The initial terror of nuclear war that had promoted Rock and Roll to revolutionary status involved a battle with nuclear governments and armies. An involvement with atmospheric pollution and waste disposal could be conjoined with far less self-pollution. Joining the tribes of motorway blockers and calfophiles was a haphazard spontaneous affair in which anybody could find their own tree and build their own Wendy house up it. As with the Lost Boys, committees were rudimentary and rules non-existent. The causes were simplistic and so were the tactics. It was somewhere to go between onslaughts on Stonehenge and the sporadically surviving open air festivals of Rock and Roll. Protecting abused animals involved one in little more than visiting some nice places to voice one's own wrath. The hoarse aggressive demands of loyalty and sacrifice from a trade union structure that was in no way 'turned on, tuned in' nor 'dropped out' would no longer embarrass. It would no longer fall necessary to ask if the offered chip was fried in animal fat or not. No longer would one have to tolerate Arthur Scargill's sideburns or the pin-up girl in the mineworkers' newspaper.

Thence to the ecology of the uniquely adulated self. Still comparatively unconcerned about what drugs were doing to our synapses or EMI to our eardrums, we started to read the small print on supermarket packages, to shun dairy products, then devour them, then shun them again, to abolish tobacco, unless, that is, it had dope in it, join aerobic classes in genital-clinging garments, to wag our fuckbits about under cover of an impenetrable pretence of sexual oblivion that guaranteed, in its hammerlock of new taboos, that nobody along those gyrating ranks would touch each other or come near. No personal space so perfectly maintained as that of the aerobic class.

We got neurotic about hair, spending more on a grotesquely promoted craft, hairdressing, than we had ever spent on books, paintings, records, tapes, strike funds or one another.

Increasingly we were at pains to say to ourselves: 'The world is still damned and befouled but I am not. As the oceans rise and sunshine gets prickly I make sure I'm seen without car, on a bike, a mountain bike with a plastic crash helmet the shape of a rugby ball and a worthless face mask, the satin clinging to my parts as surely as Elvis's jeans ever clung to his. So when and if the seas run dry and skies go hot and white for mankind's last moment anybody seeing me will know that it *wasn't my fault.'*

Bradford. 1976

Gillian Clark is leaving. Her stay as Visual Arts Officer for the Yorkshire Arts Association has been short and vigorous. She has displayed a wide concern for interfusions between the local people and local artists and she has shown herself more than prepared to extend the normal boundaries of visual art to fuse with performance and theatre. She is taking over the rehoused Liverpool Academy where, under her auspices, the bar manager will run up sufficient deficit to bankrupt this historic institution and land her successor, Murdoch Lothian, with a lifelong debt.

Her farewell do is being held in an old institutional building on the Leeds Road. She is situated at the entrance, bottle in hand, to pour everyone a glass and receive their farewell prezzies as they arrive.

As I make my entrance a young woman with a lean face, a plain haircut, a plain patterned dress and no make-up stands near the drinks table. She has nothing of the dress language, the style, nor the bearing of an artist. I assume immediately that she is one of Gillian's office staff, disorientated and a little nervous amongst the freaks and the ravers.

'Jeff,' says Gillian, 'This is Jan.'

'Hello, luv,' I say and I throw an avuncular arm around her, anxious to show that I, at least, am happy to be in the company of the lay public. She throws my arm off her shoulder as though it had been immersed in rat vomit. She shudders brusquely and averts angry eyes.

'Whassamatter luv?' I say. 'Don't you like being cuddled?'

'Jeff,' says Gillian Clark, her voice hitting a note of steely urgency. 'Get to the other side of the hall now.'

'What the fuck's going on?' I ask, genuinely bewildered.

'Don't ask questions,' she says. 'Go!'

I take a bottle from the table and go. I sit somewhat puzzled and disconcerted in a remote corner of the premises. I spot Di Davis, a performance artist of particular inventivness whose work I've admired for some time. 'Di', I say, 'I've been banished to the shadows.' 'Don't cause trouble,' she says.

Some time later in the evening I return to the booze table to ask Gillian Clark for some explanation.

'Jan is a radical feminist working with the General Will,' she says. 'If you go near her after having touched her the way you did there's likely to be violence. Now please stay clear of her or go.'

I do not. I demand an explanation from Jan. In minutes I am surrounded by aggressive women who pin me to the wall by my shoulders and accuse me of everything but the then unsolved Ripper murders.

'Shit to this,' I say. 'I'm leaving. I'm going home to my wife.'

'No you don't,' says Jan. Here Diz Willis intervenes.

'You can't stop him leaving if he wants to,' says Diz.

'Keep out of this,' says Clark shoving him back.

'Who are you shoving?' says Diz and shoves her back. There is a small history here. Clark and Willis have recently terminated a short sexual relationship. Clark hits Willis. Willis decks Clark.

'Do you condone that?' asks a rouged young man, also of the General Will.

'I must,' I say. 'It was struck in my support.'

The first fist is in the gut, then a knee in the crotch. Numerous hands fling me one to the other, then hurl me to the floor. The boots and winkle pickers thump into my ribs and my kidneys. I void my bowels.

'Stand back,' says Gillian. 'Now get up Nuttall. Get up Willis. I think you'd better leave, the pair of you. You've caused enough trouble.'

I spot Di Davis over her shoulder smiling as though some special dream had come true.

PART FOUR

ADMASS

All money is dirty.

Richard Wilson, artist.

I think fashion is and always has been an
important motor force in art - if you do not
believe in the importance of fashion then you
must believe in the myth of the artist as
individual genius driven only by super-human
self-motivation.

Waldemar Januszcsak.

Der der deary didi!
Der? I? Da! Deary?
Da! Der I, dedida;
da dada, dididieryda.
Dadereder, didereader.
Dare I die, deary da?
Da dare die didi. Die
Derider! Dididwriter.
Dadadidididdada.
Aaaaaaaaa! Der I da.

Oedipal Fragment,
Terry Eagleton.

1.   GARRETS AND CATWALKS

What artist is famous compared to Burt Reynolds?
                                Julian Schnabel.

In art you can't think about money. The sensibility
and the elegance of the piece of work would be
jeopardised by that.
                                Richard Wilson, artist.

Fashion is the enemy of art. Art coins new images, sounds, frissons. Fashion trawls images, sounds, frissons. Artists despise slavish imitators. Fashion is a system of imitation, applauding the correct and up-to-date, ridiculing the incorrect and passé. Art followers seek to be astonished and disorientated perpetually in as many wayward directions as there are individuals. Fashion followers seek to find security in exact conformity. Art is neccessarily non-conformist. The artist must follow his pleasure independently, unaffected by pressures of convention. Fashion is a system of competitive convention.

Fashion and art overlap. There is no doubt that the work of Picasso, Leger, Delaunay, Kandinsky all contributed to the Art Deco style. There is no doubt that the work of Rodin, Böcklin, Munch, Klimt and Schiele contributed to the Art Nouveau style. It can't be denied that within the Paul Whiteman Orchestra there was Bix Beiderbecke. Fred Astaire was no ordinary hoofer. Charles Rennie Mackintosh was no ordinary furniture designer. Within commercial genres Raymond Chandler, J.G. Ballard and Ernest Haycox manage to be considerable artists. A recent exhibition at the Barbican Centre called *Jam* demonstrated the counter-fusions. Nonetheless, although appearances between art and fashion may be similar or even exactly the same, art is governed by the urge to examine and extend human sensibility, and fashion is governed by the urge to control and exploit it. Art gives out of courage. Fashion takes out of fear.

The artists making their bid to take over fashion as a vehicle for spreading a positive sensibility that could possibly save the world were, as we have seen, nave about the subtlety, the power and the irresolvable different nature of fashion. In 1967 and '68 it looked as though art was indeed infiltrating and invigorating simplistic popular forms. In the TV serial *The Prisoner*, disjointed ambiguous narrative juxtapositions got onto popular TV. Zappa and the Pink Floyd brought Stockhausen and Cage into the rock dance scene. By 1980, however, it was quite clear that art had not usurped fashion to create an explosion of released mind. Fashion spread, curled at the edges and enfolded art, so that now, under the Rock and Roll Dome, the idea that fashion and art vary in any way invokes jeers of ridicule.

We were very preoccupied, in the early years, with the consciousness called 'hip'. Hip was a black jazz term and originally it meant 'aware'. For instance it was possible to use it quite literally. If someone said: 'D'you know we're late?' the reply might be: 'Yes. I'm hip' meaning 'Yes, I know.' 'Get hip to this' meant 'Learn this.'

Hip, in jazz, was exclusive. The implication was that not many people were hip. Jazz, by the late thirties, had become a complex and difficult art, a field in which the old 19th Century bohemian ethic of following the muse rather than playing to the gallery, of ostentatious poverty in pursuit of the incomprehensible, prevailed. The leaders were 'far out', which is to say they had reached a distant region beyond common understanding. They were 'out to lunch' which meant that they were not available for communication. Few people could follow the extraordinary improvisatory techniques of Charlie Parker and Clifford Brown. The few who did were hip. Those who did not were unhip.

Hipsters, particularly the artists, used drugs, particularly marijuana, heroin and benzedrine. The 'far out' place that had been reached by soaring musical vision and

Danny Barker and Dizzy Gillespie by Milt Hinton.
... the loose-fitting suits, the wide-brimmed pork-pie hat, the vivid tie ...

Lester Young.

unprecedented instrumental brilliance was equated with the 'far out' place reached by drugs, erroneously as the dying Parker was at pains to point out.

Rock and Roll, quite rightly, considered hip to be elitist and certainly the bebop bandstand was the most savagely competitive arena where only the aristocracy survived. The jazz hipsters had signalled their awareness by a kind of uniform, the cool, loose-fitting suit, the wide-brimmed pork-pie hat, the vivid tie, a style probably set by the great saxophonist Lester Young. When a minority espouse a uniform the swift impulse is to accrue credibility by watching what the hip are wearing and to emulate it. Thus a mark of exclusion becomes a fashion and the unaware are claiming, by dress, an awareness they'll never share.

The Rock and Roll world rightly proclaimed that clothes and drugs were more democratic than instrumental skill, acute musical awareness, or dedication. They created a culture in which the universal style became exclusive and the exclusive style universal. A whole generation was hip, followed by another, and yet another - hippies, yippies, punks, acid house ravers - from whom the central focus of hip, difficult revolutionary music, had been forgotten. The moment is not far off when the little red ribbon will be sported by people who have little idea what AIDS is. Some already believe AIDS itself to be fashionably desirable as they believed suicidal heroin addiction to be fashionably desirable. A culture which despises facts has little real appraisal of mortality. If the price of admittance to victim culture is to demonstrate that you are a victim of the straight world then being an AIDS sufferer or a heroin addict ranks high as an impressive qualification. Infected rent-boys biting and spitting at arresting officers deploy their disease as a vengeful weapon. At the time of writing the hoardings are blatant with five new, emaciated, near-dead sociophobic role models advertising Danny Boyle's film *Trainspotting*.

It was a favourite stance of self-trained jazz musicians and politically alienated beat poets to use hip as a whip to flog the orthodoxy. Eggheads had acquired their brilliance by good fortune or by discipline. Here was proof that vision and genius had

Hot Lips Page.

a pre-educational vigour, an access to excellence based on inherited awareness and mutually nurtured skills. It seemed a much-needed proof that creativity is rooted outside the socio-political structure, that here was art in the full sense, a position of integrity from which the warmongering establishment could be attacked and healed.

But when hip moved from the hipster to the hippie, when the right clothes and the right drugs raised the world to a hubris of historical ascendancy, art and genius needed to be swept aside along with academic orthodoxy. Our jubilant vengeance against the eggheads spread like HIV to include a blasé contempt for difficulty. Art went out of the window. 'Boring' became the ready-to-hand term of dismissal where 'Bourgeois' had once been the cry. In the British art schools, which continued, until the mid-Eighties, to be the hothouses of cultural transformations, the bearded and corduroyed agents of initial information found themselves dismissed as 'boring old bohos' and jazz itself was ultimately ditched as 'a lot of old men in baggy suits smoking cigarettes.' There was even a band in Liverpool called Johnny Hates Jazz, whilst, in the perceptive film *The Commitments*, the Judas in the soul band who betrays his commitment is the guitarist who breaks out of the three-chord corral and heads for the hills of jazz harmonics.

The paint-spattered bohos in the art school staff were briefly amazed and gratified to be confronted with a student body that seemed to have left them behind. It was only in the mid-Eighties when the tools of fabrication (such as brushes and chisels) went down and the chairs encircled into a debate of suspended certainty that the disease could be identified.

Meanwhile fashion provided a substitute for the artist. The licence, esteem and special mystique previously afforded to figures like Sartre, Picasso, Breton, Dylan Thomas, Charlie Parker, or Allen Ginsberg was now reserved for securely vacuous millionaires like Michael Jackson, Courtney Love, Kurt Cobain and Madonna. In fact the pathetic Jean-Michel Basquiat whose soporific doodles died a protracted death in the shallows of a barely recollected tradition, declared bitterly to Madonna, his occasional lover, that he would rather have been a rock star.

Eggheads had emerged who, in pages of acrobatic opacity, in a new mutual jargon which granted their discourses a fake aura of exclusive intelligence (flattened fifths of the seminar) denied the possibility of any individual transforming the culture by introducing new perceptions. When Lacan, Derrida, Foucault, Barthes and Althusser rubbished the model of history as a list of the names of innovators, those who had already rooted their standpoint in the study of, and the conformity to, fashion, gladly embraced this sublimation of their idleness.

Conviction (information that's found, grasped and suffered through a passionate intensity of pleasure with all its taxing demands) may now be evaded. No longer need we involve ourselves in fatuous self-sacrifice, the soaring trajectories, the smashed hearts, the brutish despair. We may now examine modes and patterns of bonding, dipping a finger in here, a prick in there, choosing a tactical childbirth at a time determined by career, never allowing the turbulent imperatives of adoration to muddy our personal space or our blind self-regard.

No longer need there be the degree of religion that compelled the individual into meditation or prayer. It became far wiser to study comparative religions, choosing, perhaps, a little Buddhism here, should marijuana favour it, a splash of Calvinism there should feminism find it useful, with a clear escape route back to agnosticism if freedom, isolation and lethargy are ever once threatened. In art the quality masterwork became questionable. When the culture is being studied rather than moulded, mediocrity is as valid as genius.

Finally, the class of '68, admittedly a group of academic Marxists who had been at the forefront of the May conflagration when the whole world-delivering strategy came to a premature peak and failed, found, in their defeat, the demise of Modernism.

The Post-Modernists, restored to their recently occupied seminar rooms of Nanterre and the Sorbonne, believed, with foggy correctness, that '68 had indeed been the testing point of philosophy going back to Kant, Hegel, Rousseau, De Sade and Nietzsche, politics going back to Robespierre, Tom Paine, Benjamin Franklin, Marx and Prudhon, art going back to Beethoven, Wagner, Turner, Blake, Larmartine, whose failure constituted a cancelling out of philosophy, politics and art. Structuralists, with their Marxist egalitarianism, had already binned philosophers, politicians and artists, handing the tools and the rewards to somebody called culture. Post-Modernists Lyotard, Deleuze and Guattari happily recognised the emergence in society of nomadic groups called rhizomes, non-domestic cultural formations who were trans-national, bisexual, free of the previous moral mandates and historic determinants, unaware of meta-narratives, mobile in a political and critical void, aficionados of Nietzsche and De Sade. Just who were rhizomatic and who were not

83

remained as amorphous a tenet as just what modernism was, but it seems that the new jet set, Sarne's Marie Claire (so soon to become a magazine), sweaty biker tribes, Kathmandu-bound hippies, inner-city street gangs and drug smugglers were all fair candidates bound together by the common factors of drug use and Rock and Roll. However rhizomatic they may have been they were prisoners under the intellectually sealed Rock and Roll Dome.

History, such as it remained, was to be understood by the study of rhizomatic patterns of culture as they emerged. The ball was exactly where we wanted it, in the court of the mindless where we could keep it safe from genius and insight.

Baudrillard was soon to follow. He snatched up the ball and placed it where Marshal McLuhan had pitched it thirty years previously. History, such as it survived, was not a matter of emergent tribal culture; it was inevitably and forever to be found in a fusion between money and technology. Humanity's future belonged to the media and market demand which constituted the only reality.

Here he struck an extraordinary affinity with Richard Dawkins who postulated the meme. The meme is any powerful and influential cultural ikon, from the British bulldog to the nipple ring. Dawkins granted it parallel power to the gene which as he eloquently points out, is for continuum but not concerned with progress. Thus, importantly, its significance lay in its amoral power rather than in whatever ethical, aesthetic or mimetic merit it may have. A meaning as loose as that of the original CND symbol or as void as the ticks and insignia shaved on the scalps of young London black men, or the strange syllables they aerosol in vivid splendour on the walls of London railway cuttings, may all operate more efficiently in promoting the vigour of social groups who have become hostile to burdensome meaning. Who could have foreseen that the Big Mac and the Coca-Cola logo would wield more power than the hammer and sickle or that a crass plastic monument to Michael Jackson would replace Prague's Lenin in bronze? Memes indicated how the media could retain power while abandoning all contacts with politics or ethics.

The word Media was, until the Seventies, the plural of Medium, which meant an intermediary means. One communicated, for instance, by the medium of the penny post, or by the medium of the Morse Code, or by the medium of semaphore.

The promotion of the plural first took place in art when artworks that partook of music, theatre, sculpture, such as happenings, assemblage, dance and costume, were described as mixed media. After Marshal McLuhan media meant radio, video, TV, fashion, discs, tapes, tabloid press, magazines and computers which proliferated in the Sixties and Seventies with the steep acceleration in electro-technology.

As we excused the stars from the limitations we imposed on the pest of humanity, so we excused electronics the limitation we imposed on science and politics. Even at the height of the Digger survival when the disciples of Emmet Grogan were dropping out into Drop City, where the way of life was based, more or less, on the iron age culture of the Apache and the Yaqui, nobody ever managed to recapture acoustic music as the sound of celebration. Reed pipes, cigar-box fiddles and bongos were played into state-of-the-technology sound systems. The cracked tones of the shaman and the street blues singer were howled through massive amplifiers.

The naivety with which computers, word processors, colour TV and synthesisers were all embraced as liberators, as media developments that could restore power to the people, remains to this day. The notion that the media were, in themselves, a new means, not of communication but of massive control, that the outcome of elections and murder trials are now decided by TV coverage and banner headlines that have become increasingly moronic, is completely lost by Baudrillard, in whom ethics are all but suspended anyway. The triumphant crowing of Internet surfers about the revolutionary evasion of political control made possible by their twinkling little screens are not threatened by truth. Their exchanges have no access to verification. Anyone can get away with any lie. Nor is there any fear that this is a kind of Wild West of culture, where psychopathic drug barons, pornographers and jungle-industry multinational slave-masters may also evade that political control. It is ironic that political control suddenly re-emerges as the sole means, not only of saving the world, but of saving those qualities of human progress that make world-salvation desirable anyway.

For the digerati are able to take a distaste for fact and a lazy evasion of thought into a starry-eyed and militant pursuit of a world-wide system of fiction. Total amnesia is permitted whereby the actual world, particularly the self, becomes irrelevant. Cybertechnology has become like language as seen by Derrida. It has become pre-creative existence, the destiny of young people, who have lost all their initial pleasure.

Virtual sex is perhaps the most pathetic example of Virtual Reality because, unlike real sex, it is safe. Virtual Reality, in the cyber-world, is held to be equal and, in most ways, superior to the factual. The marauding wonderstruck human with his tumescent senses has been abandoned in favour of membership of a hive where all functions must be learned, but none chosen, and where the hectic range of pleasures that can be made to play on the human skin (seen in the cyberworld as a problem) is gladly and easily forgotten because, under the Rock and Roll Dome it had already been so much diminished; the voluptuous painting of Titian and the grain of medieval carving, the dew on the meadows of the Usk and the odours of a lover's garments, are replaced and reduced to electric light in a lounge-lozenge. The future, which has been hailed like a messiah by evangelists such as Nick Land and Sadie Plant, (employed, to their temporary embarrassment, in midland universities) and by Kevin Kelly (who edits the cyber-magazine *Wired*) is reduced to knowledge (postulation) which is prone to error or misrepresentation, has lost experience (demonstration - initial information) which is not vulnerable in the same way. It is forgotten that the copper wire must be mined and manufactured, the plastic boxes designed and moulded out of materials whose source is still agricultural, like the food that keeps the cyber-surfer at this keyboard and the girders and timbers that support the space in which he operates. The cyber-facilitated media chat merrily about a sanitised, smoke-free post-industrial consumer society while our tycoons produce our consumer goods under ceilings of dense green foliage a long way away, so that we may ignore the ever necessary manual work that is done by a peonage of jungle folk who escape to a better life in the sex industry if they're lucky. Crusaders of cyber-culture, many of them one-time Socialists, call our era post-industrial, and our society post-political, uncaring about the way in which computers have enabled industrial predators to sidestep the unions and the law. The intonation of the digerati is familiar. It is the weary superciliousness of the 'tuned-in' (Internet is awfully close to the druggy global consciousness). Thatcher's children, they have no recoil from the uncontrolled capitalism that sells drugs and children's genitals as well as anything else along the network. Consumer exploitation is the condition of humanity. For them the word 'market' is a synonym with the word 'express'. Consumed with *jouissance* you no longer cry it, sing it, nor describe it. On the Internet you must market it.

There is no sadness here, no sense of deprivation or crippling loss left by people who no longer make love with the needs, mutual caring, odours and mortality of salty human sweetness, but masturbate by electrode, computer regulated, while some mutation from the urban wilderness depicts itself as an erotic formulaic image. Here is friendship with no commitment, pleasure with no astonishment, destiny drained of adventure.

Completely forgotten is the loathing which the alternative culture felt for media control at the onset of the stop-the-bomb strategy. As drugs and fashion asserted themselves and achieved their triumph, so electricity was understood increasingly, not as an industrial product that could be ended by withdrawal of raw materials, but as a fact of nature, to be taken as much for granted as daylight, oxygen and sex. It was doubly odd that this phenomenological identity should be seriously afforded to electricity just as it was being denied to mortality. Increasingly the listeners or the viewers focused their pleasure on the equipment over and above the performer. That Caruso, Louis Armstrong and W.B. Yeats are just as good on scratchy 78 rpm shellac as they are on CD because they are the same is no longer understood. When Clint Eastwood made his film about Charlie Parker, great rhythm support by Max Roach, Bud Powell and Percy Heath had to be erased and replaced by a modern backing that was held to be superior because it was electronic. That the flickering black and white of Eisenstein or D.W. Griffiths has qualities that make it superior to the seamless pans and zooms of TV soap is also not understood. That the relationships in Albert Square and among the Ewing dynasty interfuse with and befoul our daily experience of our own real relationships obstructs the rekindling of any concern we may retain for the factuality of our surroundings, our appetites, our loved ones and our own authentic identities as vehicles of free and potent action.

The generations of the '30s, '40s, and '50s spent a great deal of time in the cinema. Nonetheless we emerged into the daylight and into the difficulties of our unique lives. It was on the paraphernalia and personae of these unique lives - family, enemies, lovers, rivals, assailants, friends - that our passions, griefs, loyalties and reactions were focussed. But, as the century closed, many of us were so riveted to television and the enfeebled condition it generates, that we have made the media fiction the focus of our deeper emotions. Grief and anger for paedophilia on Brookside, wrongful imprisonment on Coronation Street, chicanery on Albert Square run far deeper than the emotions we feel for those whom we have the daily opportunity to touch. Our existential motors having been thus colonised by trite fictions, we find ourselves excluded from the screen, deprived of a visible place alongside people we know far better, and care for much more deeply, than our own flesh and blood. Voyeurs we may be but, as such, we are invisible to our real loved ones. We too want to be seen up there where it counts, on screen. We want a part in the play which is so much more real to us than reality.

The death of Diana, Princess of Wales, gave us the opportunity to usurp the set. We could sign books giving us a tiny but direct contact with the Spencer family, an immortality comparable with that of the war memorial, but an immortality nonetheless, a mini-second of Warholian fame. We could hurl flowers contributing to a colour-scrambled compost-heap. We could wait in patient, silent, tearful ranks while the camera dollied alongside the gun-carriage. Pavarotti, Sting, Elton John and our gerbil-like prime-minister grieved with us, thus, for once sharing the screen with us. Some of us actually got to stand really close to them, on camera. The mythic attributes of saintliness, martyrdom, and marital victimhood, fanned to white heat by the tabloids, licensed us to usurp the ceremony until the real star of the event became the snivelling British public.

As the hearse crawled through North London, the movement of the crowd across the passage of the cortége and the blocking of the windscreen with more and more wilting bouquets, indicated the surly reluctance to end the day by the simple planting of a fatal road-casualty in an ordinary grave. For a moment or two, as the coffin passed through Brent and Willesden, there seemed a passing danger that we might stop the car, seize our Princess's remains and bear away fragments of her cadaver like Scottish football fans bore away hunks of the Wembley turf in '76.

Elizabeth II could scarcely be blamed for failing to realise that the media, governed by nothing more than Mammon, protected by nothing more than crass capitalist exploitation and subtle Post-Modernism on the part of the media administration, had attained power of infinitely greater strength than our Monarch or her elected government.

Politicians and premiers have not commonly been speakers at Royal funerals, but Blair, doctor-spun, knew that the Windsors and the Spencers were not the real hosts here. The host was Mammon to whom Blair had promised the nation's soul.

2. LARCENIES

Many things will emerge that we, as mere neurones
in the network, don't understand, can't control.
But this is the price for an emergent hive mind.
                                                       Kevin Kelly, ed. *Wired*.

It is frequently argued by those who wept at the moon landing and those who believe the Internet to be a common mind, like the one we shared when stoned, that we are all in the midst of a massive transformation in our own functioning on Earth. This is no longer technology, the instrument of human choice and intention. This is the manifestation of some overall humanity previously incapacitated by the limited means of humanity's infancy. Nave optimism is always touching, whether seen in the eyes of the starving Irish bound for New York, the zonked-out kids hitch-hiking to Tibet, or the tone-deaf expressing themselves on untuned guitars. All that we have to work with is the real. Ideas will not keep us warm, keep us fed, reproduce us, cure our physical afflictions nor fuel our electrical services unless ideas are compelled by real instincts and have real materials with which to work. The only ideas of any worth are the ideas that serve and manipulate facts.

Ideas, then, which have a root importance in our further well-being are ideas about the provision and distribution of materials whether they be coal, oil, uranium or copper. The set of ideas we have fallen back on in the massive mishandling of our attempt at revolution, is not new at all. It is called capitalism. Behind the idea of capitalism lie the ideas of greed, fear, and isolation. These are the ideas we grasped when we opened our arms to embrace generosity, love and mutuality. When we resign our identities and their powers of experience we donate ourselves to anyone who wishes to exploit us.

Capitalism holds that greed is a constant natural element, a real instinct indeed. In this belief capitalism makes no distinction between the true basic drives of self-preservation and self-protection and the destructive perversion of these drives into competitive self-gratification. The game has always been the same, say capitalists, and always will be. Standards of real good and bad are, to capitalists, measured only by success or failure in the competitive field of self-gratification. Capitalism has, for centuries, maintained an uneasy partnership with religions preaching self-denial, like Buddhism or Christianity, craftily spotting that the more that is denied the masses by the masses, the more is up for grabs by the entrepreneur. In the current situation, if you have an anti-monetary ethic amongst popular musicians you don't have to pay them much.

In the light of this capitalist belief it is interesting to note how quickly capitalism panics when its control is threatened. For a group of people who believe humanity to be condemned to a Valhalla of the buck they are extraordinarily insecure, as kings or priests. In these days, however, capitalism, although not unfamiliar with the cruder means such as bombs, guns and censorship, are finding techno-cultural outflanking a more effective means of cancelling our threats to their hierarchy. If you can synthesise hegemony with monopoly, blood may not longer be necessary.

In the last decade of the Twentieth Century it seemed that capitalism had done away with the nonsensical altruism called Marxism. So towering an opposition did Marxism once seem that capitalism is now resting in a sickbed of historical inevitability, freed of the necessity to debate with Marx and able, for the moment, to deride debate itself, as all the drones buzz into line, among them Tony Blair who says 'future' all the time, but really means computers, the only future he can accept.

Capitalism in the USA has gone one step further. Shortly before the surrender of Russian Communism, not to tanks and bombs but to memes like Coca-Cola, MacDonalds and Mickey Mouse, intelligent agents of capitalism on Wall Street, in the CIA and on Madison Avenue, had spotted that the standing enemy of all established power groups is art. The outflanking of Russian popular culture had been a simple thing. Their paraphernalia of self-denial makes a dreary lifescape when set against Hollywood, Linda Lovelace and fast food. But the Russian Communists had embarked bright with art - Mayakovski, Block, Shostakovitch, Mussorgsky, Rimski-Korsakov, Eisenstein, Pevsner, Tatlin, Kandinsky, Mandelstam, all of whom they were happy to use for their kick start but whom they censored into suicide, exile, or mere obscurity, because they saw, like Plato, that artists make stormy seas on which to stabilise. 'Every artist takes it as his right to create freely, according to his ideal,' said Lenin. 'There you have the ferment, the experimenting, the chaotic. But of course we are Communists. We must not drop our hands into our laps and allow chaos to ferment as it chooses. We must try consciously to guide this.' Thus they robbed their society of its glamour, alienated their young, and finally gave in without so much as a game of conkers to transatlantic self-gratification.

In doing so they fed the argument of the engaged artists. The imprisoned poets and painters of Russia became emblems for the intolerability and the invincibility of creative freedom in the face of the State.

Perhaps the first and most bewildering strategy of the capitalists was to see the danger of making your subversives into heroes of the enemy, just as the Russians had made Solzhenitsyn and Voznesensky heroes of the West. Before the Communist bloc could make hero-martyrs out of Kenneth Patchen, Nelson Algren, Charlie Parker, Charlie Mingus, Norman Mailer, William Burroughs and Allen Ginsberg, it was necessary to nab them first and make them beacon figures of competitive individualism. The notorious link between the Pentagon and the Museum of Modern Art, and the invitation of Norman Mailer and Duke Ellington to the Kennedys' tea parties in the White House, were the first measures of this strategy, as were the creation of Arts Council stipends to the British underground. Structuralists and Post-Modernists in the Seventies, Eighties and Nineties were quick to use these events as evidence of the true nature of the work, that action painting was, after all, only icing on the capitalist cake, that the subversive avant-garde was only the play area of Spock's liberal spawn. Such a dismissal failed to take into account the existential nature of the artefacts and the difference between transformation and misrepresentation.

So important does emasculation by misrepresentation become in these capitalist strategies, it's worth sketching the rudimentary groundwork of what constitutes the reality of human arts and artefacts.

If a man walks down a street wearing a brown suit with his left hand in his pocket, with a mannerism of dragging his left instep, whistling Yesterdays, on Sunday, to buy a paper and a packet of cigarettes, then if he repeats the act with the same clothes, same mannerisms, same tune, on Monday, to rape the female attendant in the newsagents, the difference between these two seemingly identical acts is existential. Similarly the act duplicated in a police re-enactment, although nearly perfectly similar, is existentially different, the purpose of one being crime and the purpose of the other being punishment.

Similarly if a girl uses a crucifix on her necklace to pick her teeth, and someone says 'Excuse me, that's a crucifix you're abusing,' to which the girl replies 'Well it's a toothpick now' - the girl is right. She has made and endorsed an existential transformation. But if that someone now says 'So it never was a crucifix', it carries no authentic content of religious passion; it's magical significance is spurious' - that person is using the transformation to misrepresent the crucifix. If his misrepresentation is political it may be difficult for the crucifix to be restored to its original existential nature.

Similarily, if someone paints a man in formal dress with an apple instead of a face in order to challenge the materialism of warmongers and drive them mad, that image takes its place in an existentially different situation from the one in which it appears when another man takes exactly the same image and uses it to startle a jaded consumer public into buying carbonised apple juice. If, at a later date, a subsequent generation lose their ability to read the existential nature of that image, to recognise a brilliant imaginative subversion made between two catastrophic mechanised wars, then the image has lost its nature and its value and, indeed, all value has probably escaped human usage because the sensibility the artist addressed originally has become insensitised, numb: dead cells.

And finally when the Pentagon, the CIA and the Museum of Modern Art colluded to use the painting of Pollock, Rothko, Motherwell, De Kooning, as capitalist propaganda they didn't ask the artist. They transformed art into propaganda which art can never wholly or even mainly be. The designer can be relied upon to deliver the required image. The artist cannot. If a designer (or a propagandist) decides to transform an artwork into design or propaganda a vital defining element in art's existential reality is suspended, lost and maybe damaged. Society is damaged by it, and was surely already damaged to tolerate it.

The militant artists of the Twentieth Century have never, for very long anyway, harnessed their work to a political or commercial body. Internationally they have been pitted against power-structures seeking to stabilise their societies. Mayakovsky, Guillaume Appollinaire and Arthur Miller were all pitted against the artificial solemnities of war, throwing their support behind revolutionary military forces only until they spotted the corrupting, confining and devitalising elements in the new organisation. The artists of New York and San Francisco during the heroic period of action painting were near psychotic with their loathing of an international establishment which they identified with World War II, the Nazi holocaust and the H-bomb, an establishment which they saw locked in mutual suicide. To use their work in support of one of the participants in the suicide pact was gross misrepresentation. Their works, however, are art. They exist and retain their potency in the aesthetic dimension from which their power will radiate long after the nations that mis-used them have dissolved, provided people retain the ability to experience them. They, like all art, demonstrate that the eternal fact in human (and any other) nature is not property, nor power, but energy and the feeding of energising experience to the culture, a process which demands mobility in its channels of play. Art perpetually re-wires society whether anybody wants it or not. If society refuses it or loses the ability to react to it, that society forfeits its own energy and will die.

3.   THE IMAGE BRANTUB

Madison Avenue developed a powerful, destructive, decadent and abusive understanding of the image in the late 20th Century. Imagery, like cunt in a brothel, was anybody's. The profound love of sacred humanity that enabled Michelangelo to form the Rondanini Piet was just one among many notions the image may serve, as advertisers saw, public relations officers echoed and Post-Modernists condoned. Lipstick would make it a homosexual joke instead of a homosexual prayer. War-paint and an arrow could transplant it to the Little Big Horn. This was fine while the vitality of Michelangelo continued to burn, but imagery had fallen into the hands of people who had no more respect for it than a pimp has respect for women's delicate and miraculous reproductive systems. Not only may the fire die but the fire must indeed be put out, or love and beauty might re-ignite human mutual regard and all the digital drones might drop out of line in the cyber-hive. The cash flow might be blocked unless creative imagery is emasculated. An existential transformation achieves exactly such an emasculation.

Simultaneously Marshal McLuhan, making heavy claims for the historical importance of mid-century popular culture, aided by the growing predominance of found objects and other installation techniques in art-making, was able to say in the late Sixties 'Art is anything.' If art is anything, then it was a very short side-step to proclaim it nothing. Capitalism, newly promoted in its consumer proliferation, had found a way to hamstring its internal opposition.

With the instinct of a well-trained predator the capitalist had spotted how art, in the urgency of its gradual pilgrimage into the delirious aesthetic wilderness outside the city wall of the consensual paradigm, in the angry panic of its assault on a society that had redesigned itself as a scene from a Western, had laid its materials wide open for theft.

Formalism, the art which abandoned illusionistic conjuring to emphasise the qualities of its materials, had been happy to join hands with design. It was part of the Bauhaus message that the coloured planes of Mondrian and Kandinski would enhance and refresh the public sensibility if applied to wallpapers and fabrics. It was believed at Leeds, during Harry Thubron's time of influence, that working people with an artisan heritage, plasterers, weavers, carpenters, masons, had a special intelligence of the senses that would make them adept in aesthetics freed of the storytelling function. But before either Bauhaus or Basic Design, Dada, in its crazy anguish, had seen that all things are beautiful. What they did not see is that if a bottle rack may accrue the same value as a Rodin, not only does it make a small explosion in the pomp-and-ceremony of art-as-refined-taste, it also enables the entrepreneur to buy a toasting fork in Lewis's, stick it on a plinth in a gallery and sell it for the price of a Rodin maquette. That which was aimed at unseating the king, or, at any rate, the Lord Mayor, also enabled the spiv.

And in the design department the quick way in which the mobile sculptures of Alexander Calder spawned an industry in utterly banal pendulous decorations indicated what happened to material stolen by people who lack the artist's special ability to deploy it. For it is a fact that Calder's art, whilst being slight and charming, is nonetheless very good slight and charming art because it is made by an individual who has perceived a possible delight and embodied it in a fabrication, whilst it is also a fact that the endless gift-shop mobiles it made possible are not so made and scarcely yield the delight of a lollipop.

When the skill transforms itself from the depictive imitation of objects to the skilful juxtapositions of colours, spaces, materials and found objects, the public, temporarily at least, will lose its power of assessment. When people, sacrifice their power of assessment before it has caught up with a change in art skills, then the crass

Yellow Accompaniment. Wassily Kandinsky, 1924.

Cathedral of Socialism. Lyonel Feininger, 1919.

Walter Gropius Bauhaus Dessau 1925-6.
... the art which had abandoned illusionistic conjouring -
had been happy to join hands with design - ...

inherits a kind of democratic equality with the superb.

When the poet exploits ambiguity and syntactical rhythms to the exclusion of precise description and lucid narration, the same thing happens. Such prose and such verse may well find itself stolen from the delirium of revolution and redeployed in the delirium of consumer marketing. The subversive cut-ups of Tzara and Burroughs resonated richly through the world of pop music and computers.

Artists, whose task it is to present facts, works that actually do energise as surely as medicine heals, have moved to such extremes that their meanings have not securely reasserted themselves, and have been usurped by those who believe that meaning and its burden, which is truth, is so discredited that anything may be used for any purpose, however opposite to its nature.

Perhaps an early manifestation of this bland liberty was the game of football played by two Bradford schoolboys with a human head they'd acquired from the local cemetery.

The scene was set for the spin-doctors.

The Bridge by Joseph Stella.

4. POP

> The reason I'm painting this way is that I want
> to be a machine.
>
> Andy Warhol.

In the face of the massive growth of capitalism, together with the massive proliferation of its forms, inventions and manifestations which coincided with the growing militancy of art, artists were bound to drag the forms of industry, technology and the

94

... Incorporated the applied forms of capitalism into the scourging of urban society... Dawn Marries Her Pedantic Automation George III Georg Grosz

Max Beckman. Der Traum.
... phantasmagorias of contempt ...

media into their vocabulary, first in order to depict what they were attacking.

In his lengthy innovatory novel *USA*, John Dos Passos chopped up news accounts, political speeches, slogans and advertising material to give a patchwork panorama of the loathsome that he could use as punctuative passages between the chapters of his book about the failure of the American labour movement.

Federico Garcia Lorca, T.S. Eliot, Edith Sitwell and Kenneth Fearing all wrote long poems in the Twenties and Thirties describing the horror and the impending wholesale destructiveness of the fast-developing megalopolis. Georg Grosz set his suppurating capitalist monsters atopple in a cacophony of city forms, redeploying the collage techniques of other Dadaists and Cubists who had already inevitably deployed commercial imagery into the world of *objécts trouvés*. The Dadaists and Cubists stole the applied forms of capitalism for transformation within the scale of art aesthetics. Grosz did not steal them for re-use. He incorporated them as identificatory tags into the scourging of urban society as did the satirical collagist Heartfield. They stood, at that time, alongside the sick hatred of Otto Dix and phantasmagorias of angry contempt by Max Beckmann. The cacophony of nightmare skyscrapers and dehumanising electro-technological forms appeared in Fritz Lang's movie *Metropolis*. In this pointed anti-capitalist, anti-industrial masterwork humanity survived underground like Christians in the Catacombs. Much later, during the Paris riots of '68, one of the most telling of the Situationist graffiti was 'UNDER THE PAVING STONES, THE BEACH.'

The city hellscapes of Grosz and Lang were, however, very close in appearance to the celebratory cityscapes of Marinetti and Severini, of metropolitan optimists like Americans Demuth and Stella. A section of the artist body had found the ignition of crude new delight in the efflorescent commercial culture. Even in music there was the appropriation of industrial sounds. Engine whistles and rattling tracks were sewn firmly into the sound vocabulary of jazz. An eccentric called Moondog busked the New York streets echoing their sound with his home-made instruments of city junk.

The determination to embrace and create within the real contemporary urban environment, rejecting contemptuously all romantic nostalgia, all pining for lost mountains, prairie and uncluttered skies that informed a good deal of so-called non-figurative art, lay behind pop art when it arrived in the Sixties. Rosenquist, who enlarged the crass image of gaudily painted Heinz spaghetti to the scale of a Communist mural, stated that he painted to 'stop the sky coming in at the window.'

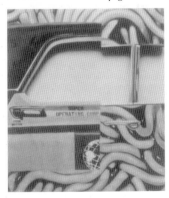

...To stop the sky coming in at the windows ...

Nonetheless this embrace was a bitter one. That windowful of sky had to be resented with a militant rigour. The British pop artists Peter Philips, Derek Boshier and David Hockney all had a pronounced acidic sick element in their early work which was carried on in the unrelenting sado-masochism of Chicagoan Ed Paschke and the dying Mickey Mouse whimpers of Jean-Michel Basquiat. The music was bitter, made by artists who knew it was bitter and knew there would never be sweetness again. Lichtenstein's jokes about art, for instance his repainting of a Picasso in comic book colour dots, indicated that a body of very capable artists had lost their regard for imagination, vitality and fecundity. Just as surely, the fragments of adolescent love-agony in his speech balloons ridiculed adolescent myths of love and, indirectly, love itself. Here were artists whose grip on reality, that is whose experience of the conditions of compelling passion, pleasure and beauty, was dim if not totally faded. The bitter surrender to the capitalist environment had involved an ethical and aesthetic abandonment which quickly fed and was nourished by the free interchangeability

Roy Lichtenstein. Woman with Flowered Hat.
... a body of very capable artists had lost their regard for imagination ...

of attitudes. Right, wrong, thriving or dying, were all goodies in the brantub. Creeds became karmas, belief became attitude (belief irrelevant). If art itself did not itself throw its defining function and self-perpetuating strength of being corrective out of the window, the pop artists certainly made art that was easy for capitalists to commercially exploit and politically emasculate. Post-Modernist irony suffered its first stirring.

Existential meaning and transformation of identical images in the different fields of satire, art and commerce itself became no man's concern. All was eventually engulfed by the gorgon of computerised PR and advertising. Rock and Roll which was the music of all young people, artists, capitalists, discontented communists, rhizomatic tribes with their universal hegemonic alternative, believed, in any case, that the attributes of integrity, subversion, power, crusading assault on corrupt established attitudes, access to original information, were now in the capable hands of stars like Lou Reed, Sid Vicious, Bob Geldof and Michael Jackson. Many artists dwelling under the Rock and Roll Dome would have downed tools immediately to become rock stars, so would quickly have substituted the qualities that aspired to stardom and hype, for integrity and creativity in their work, believing that the defining qualities of art had long ago been usurped by the pretty little talent-less stereotypical squirts who had become our main role models.

London. 1987.

It can't be as hot as Portugal was but it feels hotter. Lacking that cleansing Atlantic wind, heat gathers. The trees in the gardens of the residential streets flanking Haverstock Hill seem inflated overweighted embodiments of heat. Heat gathers around the roots of your hair and runs like some kind of oily rain down into your eyes and your shirt collar.

Coming home from a day's slog in the People Show rehearsal room in Bethnal Green, a day in which the sun belting ruthlessly down through the huge vertical windows turned the room into a sauna, Haverstock Hill has a near-tropical lassitude. The cars climb slowly, winking hot late gobs of light off their metal. People cross the road in semi-trance and cars uncomplainingly slow to let them do so.

A group of young people are assembled outside the restaurant opposite the Load of Hay. Approaching them I am amazed and a little saddened by their clothes. They are swathed in jackets, T-shirts and denims several sizes too big for them and their haircuts make them look like candidates for parts in The Railway Children, *the boys with pudding basins and the girls with tangled lilylocks. There has been a conscious de-eroticising, a complicit clinging to prepubertal codes. Gone the sporting of crotch and cleavage that was one of the delights of rock liberation. I assume them to be either pairing or buying dope. Idly curious about why they do whatever they're doing so publicly, out on the pavement rather than in the restaurant itself, I take a seat at one of the metal tables on the pavement.*

A lot has changed since I went into hibernation in my studio in Todmorden, since my attempt to turn the West Algarve into my own little Shangri-La failed so desolately. Back in London I find myself curiously unable to read a culture that has utterly transformed in the two years between '84 and '86. Standing in the bar of the Riverside Arts Centre, Hammersmith, waiting to see Ken Campbell, looking at the casually affectionate androgynes, I have already realised that I have nothing to say to these people, at least nothing they would understand or even be interested in. They have side-stepped out of my politics, my aesthetics and my sexuality.

Sitting at my table on Haverstock Hill I am surrounded by listless voices, each sentence carrying a dying fall of disdain, acknowledgement, or tempered admiration. They are lifting pieces of one another's garments and they are not looking for breasts, genitals or tinfoil packages. They are examining one another's labels. I am aware that the clothes they wear are descended from the working overalls and underwear of forty years ago, many of them with ostentatious fraying of the fabric. Cheapness and hostility to respectability were the original reasons why a socially disaffiliated generation of young people adopted them as fashion.

These clothes are expensive, however. I realise with sick amazement that sex and psychedelics have taken second place, for these young people, to competitive consumer spending. I had not realised until then the extent of the revolution's eclipse.

PART FIVE

Andy and Malcolm

Deconstruction is the death drive at the level of theory: in dismantling a text, it turns violence masochistically upon itself and goes down with it, locked with its object in a lethal complicity that permits it the final inviolability of pure negation. Nobody can 'out-left' or outmanoeuvre a Derrida because there is nothing to out-left or outmanoeuvre; he is simply the dwarf who will entangle the giant in his own ungainly strength and bring him toppling to the earth. The deconstructionist nothing lieth because he nothing confirmeth.

Terry Eagleton.

1. BREAD

London. 1958.
Bacon is showing at two galleries. At the Hanover there are more popes, more elephants, more vomiting dogs. At the Beaux Arts there is a whole new set of pictures of Van Gogh on his way to work. They are violent, immediate, unarguable and electric, every gobbet of paint, every mark charged with crucial nervous energy. There is nothing flamboyant, no compensation of emotion or voluptuousness. They are there because this is how the world, stripped of its cultural palliatives, is there for the human nervous system.

There is a mixed show at the Redfern and a mixed show at Delbanco's. I run into Bryan Wynter and later, Ed Middleditch. You always meet someone. Over a beer Bryan tells me 'Something is happening Jeff. Something is definitely happening.' And he smiles like a boy who's discovered a bright new miracle.

Saturday morning in Bond Street was a fever of young and not so young men and women anxious to catch the forward step and deal with it before we found ourselves in the dark. There was no doubt in any of our minds that value, historic value, was to be had here and not in the other areas where artists were hampered with the impediments of some industry or other.

There were alternatives, warring factions. The Redfern was losing ground it had won as the gallery representing Sutherland and neo-romanticism. Gimpel's represented French painting and what was happening in St. Ives. The dour anxieties of Soho found themselves on the walls of Helen Lessore's Beaux Arts.

Painting and sculpture was no joke, no mere pastime. It was work, it was progress, and it was the means whereby a creative mind might make a real contribution to the human situation.

Norfolk. 1976.
Early summer sits on the Norfolk landscape like a quiet decision. There are few vistas and in places on the few slopes and down the indistinguishable lanes the foliage threatens to become claustrophobic.

Three young men dressed for walking have curious headgear, something between flying helmets from the days of biplanes, and balaclavas. On the crown of each is a circular cushion sturdy enough to keep half a length of telegraph pole from settling on their scalps. There are straps, thongs and buckles for holding the pole in place as it lies across the three heads. They bear it thus as it holds them, in single file. It is bright yellow, as startling in the muted greens of the vegetation as a field of rape.

For days now these three have borne their yellow pole through Norfolk, trudging unsmiling through the villages, explaining when asked that they are Ddart and that they are performing an action sculpture. The Anglians greet them in their customary laconic drawl, extending that pokerfaced tolerance towards the eccentric that is traditional amongst them. They have a certain gratitude to anyone who does a bit of a turn to liven up the empty days. There are cups of tea, free snacks, pints, along the way.

Halfway through the week the press arrive. Someone on the Eastern Daily Press has made a bob or two by informing the nationals. The tabloids arrive, notebooks and cameras at the ready. They interview the three artists amiably and the artists are gratified that suddenly their work is in national focus.

The following day they resume the walk but things have changed. A motorist stops and shouts 'Why don't you do something useful for a living?'

At lunchtime villagers are hostile, even angry. They have read in the papers that the walk is financed by the Arts Council and that the Arts Council is financed by their taxes. A charming piece of lunacy has turned into a scandalous rip-off. They are not amused. They are cheated. Mammon swings the reading, changes the existential situation. What is seen is no longer what is meant. Inspired clowning has become audacious chicanery.

Later the Circular Walk *is used by parliamentarians to reduce arts funding. 'No money for the ridiculous,' they cry, oblivious to the fact that the humorous and outrageous art of Ddart and even Pablo Picasso must, in its nature, be ridiculous.*

Capitalism likes to think that it generates art and indeed art has been seen to thrive where money and sophistication coincide. It has also been seen to die in such places, usually where the sophistication had proved to be hollow.

Capitalism wants to believe that art is just like anything else and that artists excel by the need to outdo each other and out-sell one another. Rather is it the case though, that artists sneak in where society can afford them. That does not necessarily mean where society can afford to buy their work although that helps. It means that society has enough spare wealth floating around that it can afford to support a tiny minority of citizens who are too busy pursuing their inspiration to join in the economic effort.

From this arises the uneasy and often superficially contradictory relationship between the artist and the treasurer. The artist, in his pure function, and a part of every artist remains pure whether he knows it or not, must, by definition, be free. Some artists steep themselves in corruption, but creativity is their condition. Their flame burns like a disease and manifests itself like an accent, a religion or an old love which the artist cannot extinguish. Thus renaissance painters dawdled with their commissions. Thus Faulkner and Chandler dawdled with their Hollywood contracts. In this freedom the artist must be independent. He must be instructed solely by his muse and the instructions of his muse must be unimpeded. Early capitalists like the Medicis however, considered it their right to exert considerable control over what they paid for. Artists in their employment had to duck, dive or fly very high indeed, beyond their patrons' comprehension, to evade their control.

Later treasurers displayed the freedom of artists dwelling in their economy as a mark of prestige. This is the underlying rationale behind the sponsorship which replaces state subsidy in late Twentieth Century Britain. Thus the crazy poet becomes an eccentric national ikon on the scale of Dylan Thomas or Allen Ginsberg. Thus Goya daubed in his tied cottage, the *House of The Deaf Man*. Thus Francis Bacon's bleak monuments of elegant butchery hang in Lord Bernstein's Granada building in Manchester. Thus the Pentagon with action painting. Thus the British Council with Genesis P-Orridge

And just occasionally the treasurer, often a minor heir, himself on the fringes of the economy, acknowledges the importance of art and pays for it out of a sense of duty to humanity. Vollard thus supported the young Fauves and the Cubists. Thus Hayley supported the thankless Blake. Thus Sylvia Beach supported Joyce and John Calder supported Trocchi, Ionesco and Beckett. Thus the supportive generosity of Peggy Guggenheim and Panna Grady.

Beyond that, family and friends helped. Thus Theo Van Gogh fed Vincent. Thus the Reverend Brontë fed his scribbling daughters. And there were the art schools, the music colleges, the creative writing departments, all at one time generous with their nominal sinecures, adopting artists like others adopted African orphans and using each name and notoriety to advertise their daring, tolerance and adventurous progressive attitudes.

State subsidy blossomed briefly in the UK. Embraced with nave eagerness in the Sixties, when it was offered as an unabashed bribe to keep artists out of subversive politics, it swiftly became embarrassed by the art it supported and exerted censorship as political subsidy inevitably must.

Meanwhile some artists like Picasso and Motherwell, most of them once poor, rose to wealth through the sale of their work. Here lies the most profound flaw in the relationship between art and Mammon, because art, once bought, becomes stock and may be capitalised upon. It seems difficult to imagine that contemporary art was seldom bought as an investment until the Fifties. It is scarcely a coincidence that the sealed Dome of Rock and Roll descended at the same time. Both were an impenetrable containment of that which capitalism, or indeed any established society, hates to need – the vitality of original information. The anomalies present in the buying of art-as-investment are many, all of them traceable to a seemingly irreconcilable failure in understanding. Art does not attract price in relation to its excellence. A high price is absolutely no guide whatsoever to the success of an art work in terms of the artist's endeavour. Art is not guaranteed in its worth by a high price. Neither is its worth disproven. Enlightened art appreciation is not in the hands of a handful of hyper-aware investors. Art investors are, regretfully, almost invariably philistines to a degree. Art appreciation at the time that art is made is regrettably confined to other artists and a narrow, hip following. Art is no more measured in money than coal is measured in pints, but the purchasers believe that it is, because, at the end of the 20th Century, under the hegemony of American consumer capitalism, they believe that everything is. The totality of this error is more than silly and pathetic. It is tragic. Art is measured in the vitality, the joy and the health of the culture it feeds. Our culture is manifestly feeble, joyless and sick and Mammon is working hard at cutting off our line of recovery. Not only has the treasury ensured that art has dwindled. It has contrived to obliterate from our minds any memory of what art ever was. The glaring success of this piece of spiritual castration was initiated by a charismatic entrepreneur, Andy Warhol. Rock and Roll, with all its ramifications, made things very easy for him.

2. HERE COMES ANDY

Of all the many things that Andy Warhol might have been he was certainly no artist, unless passing himself off as an artist under the Dome of Rock and Roll counts as an imaginative act in some kind of devious way. If confidence trickery is art it is slight art. Why argue for his weevil of creative ability when Warhol was an anaconda of a speculator?

... Andy's witchboy, silver towhair, asexual, cuckoo-on-Broadway image ...
Andy Warhol photographed by Christopher Makos.

If the commercial image in Lichtenstein and Rosenquist had to be poached from the middle road between the Lower East Side studio lofts and Madison Avenue, once commercial images had been poached, gutted, expanded, distorted and hung in halls of esteem as art, a solitary figure approached the transformed image from the other side. Warhol was employed in advertising as a commercial illustrator.

In this he was not up to much. He drew lamely in a popular commercial style of the time more or less derived, ironically, from the Marxist artist Ben Shahn. Other commercial artists like Leo Baskin and David Stone-Martin drew in that style with far more skill and aplomb. Warhol, with a near supernatural insight, didn't need to learn to draw when he grasped, quite early on, indeed before anyone else, that image was free of content (the existential significance that had until Rock and Roll, been the *raison d'étre* of signification) and now enjoyed intrinsic strength. The swastika had more importance than *Mein Kampf* and could be used as a badge of anything. The fur hat and the red star had more independent significance than *Das Kapital*. The eyeliner, the hormone injection and the silicone implant had more importance than

103

menstruation or pregnancy. And Andy's witch-boy, silver tow hair, asexual, Midwitch-Cuckoo-on-Broadway image was of far greater importance than the sadistic, mother-fixated, Roman Catholic vacuity who couldn't draw that lay behind it. The day Andy realised this he must have been very pleased. He realised instantly that the veneer had become greater than the substance and began the stampede for emptiness.

Moving out of his career in real advertising into his career as a charlatan artist was, for an impersonator, a move into an area of multiple opportunity.

The events and elements which we've been exploring here combined to present Andy with a wide, albeit unidentified, field in which a gullible group of sycophants whose only security lay in belonging to a seemingly exclusive group could be marshalled to his command, in which a gullible mass of wealthy public chose to grant credibility where credibility could be measured by price.

Jasper Johns cast his beer cans ...
Painted Bronze, 1960. Jasper Johns.

Nobody knew what art was. Critics and knowledgeable collectors were buying Duchamp, only slightly confused by the fact that to invest in a Duchamp was effectively to nullify its existential nature. The same people were paying high prices for comic-strips transformed to epic canvas.

'I bet if I stuck a coupla beer cans in his gallery, Leo Castelli could sell 'em,' De Kooning had said. Jasper Johns cast the beer cans in bronze and lo and behold Castelli sold 'em. 'Aha!' said Andy.

3.   PAPER MONEY

A work can now perform its economic function
without being loved or admired: nobody need be
awakened by it, or moved by its deeper meaning.
The money pours through it like sewerage through
a drain, and the civilising function of art – the
function which justifies all this extravagance and
caused the patron to benefit from his purchase as such,
as the artist from the sale of it – has been set aside.
                                        Roger Scruton.

The spillage from depicted commercial imagery to a number of subtle reorientations of actual commercial imagery was fairly rapid. One of these reorientations was kitsch. Kitsch was a wayward mischievous delight in the tasteless. Kitsch could not be made but, like true *objéts trouvés*, just recognised. Crucifix tattoos were kitsch. Plastic quilted bars were kitsch when spotted in the front parlours of the innocent and transplanted to the lounge pads of the highly sophisticated. To bring home soup cans, plastic toys, outlandish fashion accessories and to place them on the shelf where but recently oddly formed pebbles, twisted driftwood or eroded pieces of rusty metal had lain, was to advertise a level of hip that had left good and bad taste behind. In the early Sixties a knowing class of winking and twinkling poseurs had broken through into an open enjoyment of the utterly vulgar, simultaneously demonstrating the sophistication that enabled such daring, and the innocence that was rediscovered in a childish glee at brash colours and glitter surfaces, irony in rompers.

The other aspect in the promotion of real, not depicted, commercial imagery was political in origin. The sky in the window, the pebble and the driftwood were suspect because they were rural, feudal maybe, gleanings from a bourgeois sentimentality about nature. The Castelli Gallery, Reuben Gallery, and the Sidney Janis Gallery opened their doors to an aggressively urban zeitgeist. Like Rock and Roll, with its savage contempt for the skilled or the exclusive, pop art, with its lionisation of the delinquent, the scrubber and the punk, the mechanical and the dirt cheap, joined this suddenly modish piping down the gutters wild. The authenticity

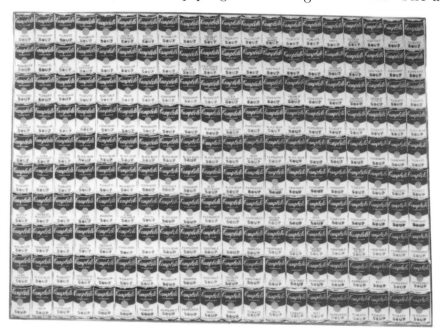

... The material for their Ceremonies ... Campbell's Soup Cans. Andy Warhol 1962

was being found that Rock and Roll was soon to call 'street'. Hip was replaced by 'street credibility', a subtle demotion.

Both avenues to the festival of junk were well favoured by the increasingly *outré* coterie of Manhattan homosexuals. Kitsch was an important part of camp, an extension of the transvestite's razor-sharp outrageousness, an ongoing thorny burlesque of stardom. 'Street' was a world thronged with tasty rough trade, a catwalk of James Deans.

What Andy had to do was promote himself by audacity and charisma, impress his street waifs, his self-isolated orphans lost in the city through drugs or onan-addiction, enslave them and persuade them to mass produce high-priced trivia in the form of prints, of printed canvasses, films, music, poetry and clothes. Andy could do with a Woolworth's blouse what Johns had done with his beer cans. Get it, hack it about a bit, sign it and sell it. Painting must be made stripped of any of the weighty baggage of creative consequence. Photographs, often stolen from the popular press or from trade catalogues, could be silk-screened onto canvas for art prices and onto T-shirts for *haute-couture* prices. If you varied the colours that would give the punters accused of buying trash (itself becoming a jargon term for a fashion quality – a subtle variation on 'street') the defensive argument that at least Warhol was a colourist.

... Art broke through in the performance skill of rock-diva Patti Smith ...

Film, for Andy, was home-movies done with an eye well cocked to the real achievements of the then thriving underground movies of Jack Smith, Kenneth Anger and Stan Brakhage. The mere fact that Warhol's increasingly powerful coterie was involved in shooting up heroin or fucking aimlessly, obsessively and indiscriminately, gave the work sufficient voyeuristic piquancy to afford some slight reward to those who dutifully endured his endless tedious hours of footage.

If here and there art broke through in this factory of art-substitute, in the songs of Lou Reed, or the poetry of Gerald Malanga, or the performance skill of rock-diva Patti Smith, that was all to the good as long as the overall quality of

... He loved to see people dying ...
Electric Chair. Andy Warhol 1965

weightless void was maintained. The pathetic dilemma of Viva fucking her dog on film, Divine eating shit on film, Joe Delissandro dying on film and Basquiat dying all over the walls revealed the uneasy truth of Andy's set-up, a sadistic scene of vertical manipulation, a cancerous Christmas tree of death with Andy as the mephistophelean fairy wielding his wand of conned bucks at the top. 'He loved to see other people dying,' said Emilo De Antonio, a visitor to the entourage. 'This is what the Factory was about: Andy was the Angel of Death's Apprentice as these people went through their shabby lives with drugs and weird sex and group sex and more sex. Andy looked and Andy as voyeur par excellence was the devil, because he got bored just looking.'

'Everyone wants to be a star.' Said Andy and indeed they did. They all wanted to be Rock and Roll stars because the Dome encompassed all, even Andy's Christmas tree. 'And everyone can be a star for fifteen minutes,' he said, thus seizing the situation that Rock and Roll had set up, in which, indeed, no special talent was necessary, only an outstanding presentational skill on the part of the presenter : Be a star. Fuck dogs. Eat shit. Shoot smack. It's easy.

Brilliantly Andy took away the gold of art which is original information, the *frisson nouveau* of Baudelaire, the Surrealism of Eluard and Buuel, the dipping rope of roccoco lace of love and despair which Charlie Parker threw out to the crowd. The wealthy have enough money. They don't go to the private view, the casino, the race meeting or the concert to be rediverted, to find true value or to be in any way interrupted in their central determination to show off to one another. Andy met this need by converting the gold to portable paper currency. 'Making money is art and working is art and business in the best art,' he said. Andy's art could lubricate the ducts of socio-sexual encounter without interruption of emotional, psychological, political, historic or aesthetic disturbance. The wealthy are not even interested in wealth. They are solely focused on one another. They find one another through avenues of barter. Andy gave them the material for their ceremonies, the dance-cards for their art ballroom, the playing cards and chips for their art poker game. It travelled lightly from purse to purse because it was weightless as a void which is what it was. Post-Modernists acknowledged him. They had, by now, taken the extraordinary stance that one element in contemporary society free of all meta-narratives, was, by virtue of its moral vacuity, money. Capitalism, lacking ideology as it did, was embraced as a possible purity. Here the irony was unconscious.

Warhol was a great capitalist. Without him humanity's corrective wisdom, art, could have survived. The ferocity that had been hurled into the Rock and Roll Dome by Dada, Surrealism and the Beats may still have survived the emasculation of commerce and mediocrity by right of Hendrix, Elmore Leonard, Bill Griffiths, Lindsay Kemp and scores of other brilliant and astute artists who kept a thread of vision and uncompromised lyric discovery sewn into the depreciating fabric of the culture.

Without Warhol the young could have been kept alert, undeceived and uncompromising, as they were until the mid-Eighties. Without Warhol, Marxism might have listened to art again and healed its diseased limb. Without Warhol, capitalism itself might have retained its deep seated patrician sense of duty to society. But Andy, without even knowing what he was doing, guided by nothing more than a ravening greed for wealth, power and fame, found art, exposed by corruption and deliberate deskilling under the Rock and Roll Dome, and he delivered it the *coup de grace*, killing the healer and laying the way clear for what was to come.

4.   TALKING IT/DOING IT

The study of an occupation has become indistinguishable from the practice of the occupation. This is a damaging confusion because the two cannot be the same. The historians and the critics are not the performers. Nor is the performer one who sits, decides on a belief, a theory or a contention, and proceeds to illustrate it. Certainly artists have passionate, even revolutionary beliefs and points of view, but these are arrived at through practice. They form their conclusions after the day's painting, the versifying, the concert, the dance. The conclusion is not the purpose which initiates the practice. The study of art deals indeed with ideas, but the practice of art does not. It is a convulsive pleasure which informs sensually, communicates sensually and only finds a cerebral level when the mind reorientates itself after the trauma of art-making. This pleasure is not an idea. It is a dilemma.

When art, then, begins to comment wryly upon itself, displaying not the acute unsparing thoroughness of committed sensibility, but displaying an ironic and distanced knowledge of its field, when it runs out of inspiration and falls back on an exchange of in-jokes between weary virtuosi, then art has indeed abandoned its factuality, its unarguable pre-social potency, and lapsed into the world of notions where it is subject to doubt, argument, ethical debate and will.

I suppose it was in the Fifties when those left-behind super-professional sidemen of the swing orchestras, the so-called mainstreamers, excused both the passion of innovation and the passion of revival, yet landed with an urbane expertise, like an aristocrat stuck with an inherited garden, started to lace their improvisations with quotes from well-known popular songs. The event, however, thus changed its existential nature, ceasing to be the 'I-feel-this-and-now-so-do-you' of the old jazz contract, and became a competitive display of familiarity with the repertoire of standard tunes and the agility to transpose them into the appropriate chord structure. The music was suddenly, for a few bars, a joke about the music.

About the same time Ornette Coleman and Charlie Mingus opened out improvisation into total expressionism, abandoning chord structures as abstract expressionist painters abandoned figuration. This was an exciting period. Brilliant young lions like John Surman and Archie Shepp were hacking wildly at the boundaries of possibility. One of the high glories of this vigorous time was the band of Mike Westbrook which could put an audience in the eye of a hurricane of convulsive creativity for hours. Critics would sneer and dismiss but they were as ineffectual in the face of this hurricane as an Oklahoma farmer confronting the real thing.

When Westbrook, in the Seventies, formed his smaller bands rendering pastiches of popular genres, a bit of Sally Army here, a spot of tango there, a perfectly rendered ragtime arrangement and so on, it was clear that a battle had been lost. The armies of revolution had stopped their assault on the boundaries of awareness and were sitting around comparing notes and showing off flashy bits of swordplay. Urgency was gone and all who preferred sport to battle heaved a sigh of relief.

A comparison between the collage style of Charlie Mingus and that of John Zorn shows a similar diminishing of aesthetic fact and augmentation of erudition. Mingus was a man driven by his own experience of long-standing interplay between the materials of his art, the resonance of gut on the sound-box plucked by a powerful male of hefty physique, the voicings of his orchestras, the significant excess of his sexuality, his political anger and his vast yearning tenderness. But, although well able to make eloquent use of expressionists like Eric Dolphy and Jimmy Knepper, he was, himself, much more than an expressionist. He used his passions to enliven his forms. In Mingus the passages writhe round one another with a supple muscularity that is only possible through real passion and the close recollection of passionate experience. The formal contrasts quiver with dramatic excitement when the music moves from one mode to another. They are the work of a man who cares about the work and the world he lives in, who posesses a depth that enhances the public importance of the work and the vigour it generates. John Zorn, by contrast, is an ironic collector. Mingus was certainly a joker too, but when Zorn leaps from Rock and Roll to rhapsody he does it as a Structuralist who doesn't believe that forms come from an individual's unique passions in a unique life. All, for Zorn, is genre which you may regard with a ludic excitement and recollective affection, but you are essentially a notator and a collector of sounds and modes. You cannot, in your own estimate, be the origin of anything. The

Jenny Holzer's Truism T. Shirt.
... the ideas are limp, half literate and tedious ...

consequence is a lowering of energy, a looseness of juxtaposition, and a sense that we are playing a clever game here rather than clawing our way through to what remains of our lives.

Pop art, as we have seen, verged happily into kitsch, celebration into collection. Conceptual art, which rigorously rid itself of all aesthetic concern and frankly devoted itself to the illustration of notions, had arrived. Insofar as nobody had stuck bald statements on a gallery wall before, this did initially seem to be innovatory enough to actually be art. It now needs vigorously stating that, however perceptive, witty or challenging it may be, it seldom is. It is illustrated opinion at best and mere opinion at its deep nadir. The exhibition has become a seminar where the ideas, free of professional testing, are commonly limp, half-literate and tedious. Jenny Holzer, Cindy Sherman and Karen Finley all exemplify this lame mode. DISGUST IS THE APPROPRIATE RESPONSE TO MOST SITUATIONS says Holzer from the depths of her wisdom. MORALS ARE FOR LITTLE PEOPLE she says. KILLING IS UNAVOIDABLE BUT IS NOTHING TO BE PROUD OF she says.

When Art-Language presented typed sheets of polemic on gallery walls as saleable art works they touched on the incantatory performance element in the

Bruce Nauman. Life Death. Knows. Doesn't Know.

lecture styles of Structuralists Lacan and Foucault. An elegant algebra of notions and ambiguous jargon had all the charm and harmless fascination of a cricket game but it had removed art from its area of demonstration. Art-Language, self-declared Marxists, soon sold to Saatchi. The games being played left the decisive battle to the stock exchange, the media and all the other cadres of Mammon. Mike Baldwin could move through complex syntax with the style of George Best. But style is not art however often it is so misunderstood.

110

5. SELLING IT DUMB

> Koons was not a commodity broker for nothing.
> He had legislated for puzzlement. He had
> engineered it. He knows its commercial value.
>
> Waldemar Januszczak

Many previously important art schools began to drift from the workshop into the seminar room in the late Seventies. Art-Language, predominant at Leeds, and feminist crusaders like Marie Yates and Griselda Pollack, were expert at luring young talents away from the aesthetic voyage to the sport of comparative theory. Art since then has been sporadic. As we have already noted, when the business is study rather than practice the bad and the mediocre are as relevant as the achieved. Indeed this is a major teaching of the Post-Modernists who were concerned to establish themselves if only to prevent modern creativity continuing to thrive. Acknowledgement of genius must cease they said, and what better way to kill it than to promote the mediocre.

Malcolm McLaren and Vivien Westwood emerged from the art school scene in the mid-Seventies. They met at Harrow. McLaren went on to Goldsmiths and Chelsea. Entrepreneurs of dislocated images, disparate style and whole card-packs of political attitudes, they would both have preferred to be rock stars but were determined to be stars anyway, and, like Warhol, they became stars anyway by finding and promoting stars. There was something almost vengeful about the way two people prevented from achieving rock stardom themselves, through lack of musical ability, should achieve stardom through their awareness that 1975 was the year to grant stardom to a band of kids who hadn't any musical ability either, even by Rock and Roll standards. The tragedy, hilarious to some commentators, was that the Sex Pistols should embody the sad inadequacy of those rock musicians who have been asked to meet the Periclean role bestowed upon them. Self-destruction became the only way in which kids with little intelligence, no literacy and nothing very much to say except 'Fuck off' could measure up to a comparison with Van Gogh, Gauguin, Rimbaud, Billie Holliday, Wols, Jarry, Modigliani, Foutrier, Charlie Parker, Dylan Thomas and all the other magnesium flares in the field of genius, in whom self-immolation was a condition of hyper-generative metabolism.

The tragedy of the Pistols was deeper even than this. They represented perhaps the last wave of young people undeceived by their mentors. Inept, illiterate and tone-deaf they may have been, but they had an ember of the authentic disaffiliation of '68 still burning in them. According to their murky lights they had a feeling that anger had been emasculated and packaged as a marketable quality and even as they cracked their narrow talents trying to reassert the unacceptability of revolt, McLaren, who knew the open scope of the market, sold them. They were the British equivalents of Warhol's streets arabs. The difference between them and Basquiat or Mapplethorpe was that the Pistols were working class cultural avengers. The desperation behind Sid Vicious's murder of his girlfriend, then suicide, was doubly terrible because he was enacting an imposed market role whilst believing himself to be a class warrior. Far from becoming a star as a result of integrity and self sacrifice, he became a star because he was void, empty and easy to receive.

The inevitability of the marketable, *star-maudit* embodied by Kurt Cobain, Courtney Love and Richie Edwards with his hacked up arms displayed to the NME could be avoided if the stars realised that a bit of musical training would be far more subversive as Mammon certainly knows and fears.

London. 1986.
The summer afternoon filters through the canvas of the marquee onto the picture hats and the floral dresses. There is a lot of jewellery made of broken glass tugging down whatever fabric it's attached to. The Ashers occupy the end of one of the trestle tables and Patrick Hughes' artist mates, Earnshaw, Baxter, Phillips, Nuttall, occupy another. A quartet of young men play a fair Louis Jordan pastiche.

Hughes is marrying a young woman whose previous partner was Vivien Westwood's brother, the unsung stalwart who spliced The Great Rock and Roll Swindle *together from a cutting room scramble that everybody else was too stoned to unravel.*

Westwood herself holds court modestly at the end of the artists' table. She is an extraordinarily plain woman with a marked Lancashire accent. Her hair is permed in a style that would have come as no surprise on the cover of the Ladies' Home Journal in 1947. Perched on top of this subtopian coiffure is a tiny velvet hunting cap held in place by a chinstrap.

The combination could not have been more hilarious if the cap had been a doll's house lavatory bowl. At any ordinary wedding it would have been a major gag causing wet legs amongst the aunts and cousins. Here no-one laughs or even affords it an untoward glance.

This is Vivien Westwood and to greet her typical cross-fusions with levity is to betray a misunderstanding of her career, her professional status and the priorities and pecking orders of the company. Discords and anomalies are no longer disruptive. They have become normal coinage.

London. 1978.
I am re-energised having just got back from a conference in Copenhagen organised by Pete Stanshill. A number of us including Rudi Dutschke, Al Alvarez and various singers, sci-fi writers and social theorists sat round and talked about 'What Really Happened In The Sixties'.
Alvarez's scepticism has been soundly shown to be negative and half informed: 'All that

really happened in the Sixties was the Vietnam War.' Michael Herr's **Dispatches** *wasn't yet out so the war couldn't be seen as a rock culture scenario.*

Dutschke was fine, bright, witty and optimistic, despite his recent recovery from a bullet in the head and his forced exile in the Netherlands.

Back in London I find myself sitting at Ann Wolff's dinner table with Gillian Reynolds and her new boyfriend, an A and R man for one of the big record companies. Every time I start to talk about the Copenhagen conference the conversation falls dead. The new boyfriend had just directed the recording of 'Bohemian Rhapsody' by Queen. He is full of awe-struck admiration for the group's co-operative professionalism, their musical skill and the seamless surface of their performance.

I try to tell him that the record immediately draws raucous ridicule in Leeds pubs. I ask him what content it has, what Galileo is doing in Bohemia with the Comedia Del Arte and Billy the Kid, what importance it has apart from being a certain seller.

'What other importance is there?' asks Gillian.

PART SIX

SAATCHI

Most of the aspiring collectors, some of whom would duly
end up on museum boards, or even with their own private
museums, could not have told you the difference between a
Cézanne watercolour and a drawing by Parmigianino.
Their historical memory went back as far as early
Warhol where it tended to stay.

> Robert Hughes.

Use your *fear* productively. Find a niche for it and
market it.

> Robin, virtual editor of ****collapse.

The claim of (Gilbert and George) being 'of their time'
has been deliberately divorced from judgement: there
is no attempt to assess their time with a critical understanding
or with an eye for what is real.

> Roger Scruton.

To have almost limitless power to call up any image, to
convey and receive information without any restraints,
to create, as it were, one's own world, would reinforce
the dangerous perception that life has no purpose
beyond individual self-gratification.

> Lord Hasgood.

1.   J.M.W. EAT YOUR HEART OUT

> Hirst's paintings are named after drugs
> and were very likely executed by an assistant:
> sometimes he paints them himself, sometimes
> he doesn't. He doesn't make a secret of this
> because the effect is the same each way.
>
>   Matthew Colling

London. 1984.

The Saatchi Gallery, Ann tells me, is in St. Johns Wood. It is not open to the public. Special permission has to be obtained if you lack an invitation from the collector himself.

We ring up. I declare myself to be the art critic of the Bradford Telegraph and Argus, make an appointment for that afternoon and off we go. The buildings are industrial sheds utterly and pointedly uncosmeticised. No colours, no banners, no embellishments. There is a fitted carpet in a neutral tone. The only sign of life is around the office by the entrance. Where the time clocks might once have stood there is a fret of efficient telephone litanies, buzzers, bells and keyboard rattle.

I introduce myself to a girl who admits me and asks if a copy of my article could be sent to them. I agree.

In the middle of one shed wall is a non-figurative canvas divided into three equal sections. Each section is a slightly different colour. The paint is smooth as print but it is paint. It is not an Albers, not a Newman, nor a Dave Saunders. On another wall is a vast Warhol on which a photograph of Marilyn Monroe has been silk-screened in rows in varying dazzle-colours. On yet another wall is a Twombly which I would admire were it not so much less than a Tapies or a Burri or a Dubuffet. Emptiness is important in this place but it is in some way different from the emptiness, the meditationary stillness, surrounding Carl André's work in the Tate.

Two young men are talking amiably in the middle of the largest shed, one of them in an open necked shirt with an expensive raincoat hooked over his shoulders. There is no-one else present.

The emptiness is exclusion, the exercise of exclusion, the almost casual registration of the power of the wealth. Ostentatious expenditure is not registered here in size and splendour. This wealth has bought space. It is the space that must be preserved, evident in its emptiness.

The *objéts trouvés* of Dada and Surrealism, the deep images of poet Robert Creeley, the non-narrative sequences of New Wave film and performance art, all of which were devised to subvert Mammon with the trauma of dislocation, were naively ignorant then, of the way or ways in which Mammon, licensed by Structuralism, catalysed by Warhol, could steal their expertise in a dislocation to stimulate the market, pulverising the selective powers of purchasers, disorientating what surviving certainty of quality there may still be, and finally ending anybody's nave belief that some brave and brilliant individuals can lift humanity above the psychopathic greed which is humanity's condition.

Both subversive forces and capitalist forces had a common interest in bypassing argument. Politicians, who continued their pretence of implementing rational polemic, refused to dismantle nuclear stockpiles or turn from their suicidal confrontations. William Burroughs attempted to implement subliminal images at the same time that advertisers were cutting them into television ads. A strong motivation from moving in on the Rock and Roll industry was to colonise advertising techniques and redeploy them in order to revolutionise political consciousness. We have seen that Mammon stole the dislocated image, guided art into the provenly impotent arena of pseudo-rational debate, redirected subversive politics into the reduced simplicities of McDworkinite feminism and Political Correctness and redeployed avant-garde material wherever they thought it would be effective, something to which deskilled ambiguous avant-garde art readily lent itself.

A vaunted semi-literacy, flattered into a heady fecklessness by wealth, toyed with vocabulary with bland disregard for its meaning or its origin. Pop videos became bran-tubs of loosely assembled pictorial fodder. Period fashions were recklessly mingled. Cod-military songs were backed by soldiers from a careless mix of comparatively recent wars. Vivien Westwood moved on from punk to a clever assembling of violently discordant garments in single ensembles: ATS corsets with Dietrich tights, Anna Neagle ballgowns with S & M collars and leather gear. The unusualness of these creations sold them. Ignorance of pre-Elvis modes is oblivious of the contradictions. The price, and the status attached to having paid it, command a deadly earnestness. No-one must acknowledge the hilarity which is the work's only possible merit. The chef whose speciality is kippers with marmalade is at hand.

The Benetton ads of Giovanni Toscani took chronically disturbing images of crude mortality, a baby spattered with the blood and slime of birth, complete with barley-sugar umbilical cord, a gaunt man dying of AIDS, and spread them over the hoardings to advertise brightly coloured woollen clothing. The true significance of such images appearing here was not the shock impact of these most private of events suddenly made gauchly public. That, indeed, was the gimmick. The true significance was the fact that the images had no connection whatsoever with the product.

Since then car manufacturers have used earthquakes, tank warfare, birth again (father passing out), intra-uterine film of embryos, any image of traumatic mortality to sell Peugeot 406 and Rover 400.

Marlboro have used desolate photographic pastiches of the work of Edward Steichen and Dorothea Lang to sell cigarettes. The selling point is to associate the product with a high quality photographic landscape. The idea that cowboys are mysteriously drawn to cigarettes named after a British Royal estate has long since been forgotten. This exploitable ambivalence of content may have been foreseen. It seemed strange in that, no sooner had Roland Barthes proclaimed a content for clothes and objects in the 1960s, than Derrida questioned a meaning for verbal language in the 1970s. Barthes, with Desmond Morris and McLuhan, was aware of what a mini-skirt was signalling. But simultaneously Derrida credited poetry with the power of generating love rather than declaring it.

Clothes and bric-a-brac, songs and slogans, logos and catch phrases were the memes, the self-perpetuating genes of culture that Dawkins was to recognise in the Nineties. But if the Crescent can still nullify Sadaam Hussein's military defeat in the Nineties, if Mrs Mopp's 'Can-I-do-you-now-sir?' contributed to the election of the Attlee Government in the Forties, this is because the content they carried was bestowed upon them by initiators and defenders, designers, entertainers, and priests who held sympathetic attitudes towards the benefiting causes.

But genes have a linear function which is the continuation of the tribes they inhabit. Were they to lose identity, as Barthes' signifying objects lost identity along with Derrida's philosophic syntax, then the species has lost cohesion. A culture relying on the power of its hoard of slogans and images to ensure its continuation is doomed, particularly if the slogans and images can be made to mean anything, as Giovanni Toscani's violent images somehow mean BUY PRETTY WOOLLENS. It will disintegrate unless art reinvigorates it. We may then see that, with a culture dissolved through the annexation of its images, we can never achieve a pre-societal anarchist paradise which was the hope of '68. For Baudrillard even anarchism is a grand narrative and it must be dissolved so that we can relax into the drone mentality and take our place in the cyber-hive whose real name is unresisted exploitation.

A most potent body of manipulators emerged in the Seventies in an unperceived new profession, long before Toscani's exemplary inanity. They were later to be called spin-doctors but then they were either called publicity advisers, public relations officers or advertising agents. Spin-doctors developed, as major movers in the making of the millennial world, because these three areas, so brilliantly analysed by Marcuse in *One Dimensional Man*, started to move together as politicians and universities started to use advertising techniques, as clothing and cars became more prestigious than brilliance and integrity, as popularity became more important than principle, as wealth became a synonym for goodness and health. Spin-doctors, empowered by ready-to-fingertip digital solutions, were able to advise on the stage-direction of debates, on the numerical desirability of photographed whereabouts, on a choice of colour, information and imagery that would obviate any necessity that once may have existed for the client to improve the human lot. They had woken up to Baudrillard's hyper-reality in which credibility had been withdrawn from the real and transferred to the fictional. A vendor wishing to sell or a political party wishing to be elected must prepare to be seen as a seductive fiction, as a star, in fact. Whatever spin-doctors call themselves the army has long had a word for what they do. They are experts in bullshit which, in the army, is spit-and-polish, a spurious façade, a false veneer, behind which all corruption and inefficiency may be concealed because, as every sergeant major knows, bullshit baffles brains. Bewitch your clientele and you will blind them to your misdemeanours, your shortcomings and your flaws, even your merits, if they concern reality. John Major and Tony Blair openly bickered about the difference in sizes of their wreathes at the Dunblane memorial service. Blair, guided by Peter Mandelson, who, in turn was guided by his pal James Palumbo, son of Lord Palumbo and director of the pop venue, Ministry of Sound, was able to continue and embellish Thatcherite capitalism simply by calling it Labour.

Spin-doctors, with all their computer technology, have unprecedented knowledge of the ignobility of the public. They are unhampered by the local greengrocer's respect for his community, by the dedicated trade unionist's love of the working class, by the progressive politician's belief in holding a positive expectation of his constituents, by the artist's belief that narrow lives may be broadened and enriched. They are untroubled by any delusion of altruism or moral optimism in or for the people they woo. They are very grateful for terms like Post Humanist, Post Modernist, Post Industrial, because such terms enable them to shrug off whole worlds of concern to which they never granted much credibility anyway. Finally the spin-doctor is unimpeded by any regard for human rights except for the right to buy worthless products endlessly if humanity so desires. He grants the buying public its every half-informed desire and only acknowledges the progressive possibilities of the public if that public can be swayed by the flattery of being so esteemed.

It was into a lake of deconstructed cultural soup that Charles and Maurice Saatchi boldly sailed in the Seventies, empowered by a childlike glee in the material with which they dealt – money. Charles was blessed with a wife, Doris, a young and smart American who had strong connections in the American art market. The Saatchis swiftly conducted PR, advertising and business consultation into a far wider area than those activities had previously presumed to occupy. Unprecedented power was achieved by taking their activities into two areas where power based on integrity had previously been expected – politics, which monitored and improved the law, and art which monitored and improved the culture or at any rate had done until Rock and Roll demoted it.

They usurped politics because Margaret Thatcher invited them to do so, appointing them official Conservative Party advisers in public relations. Art was usurped more subtely by Charles Saatchi who became such a lavish collector that his choice of purchase became hegemonic. He was the monetarist messiah to Warhol's John the Baptist.

Unlike Warhol, Saatchi had neither to disguise his art as egalitarian, anti-elitist street politics, nor as an extension of John Cage's principles of composition. Rock and

Roll had usurped, cheapened and exhausted both these energy-zones. After all, Saatchi's art wasn't by him, it belonged to him. By the time he arrived it was no longer necessary to establish street credibility or aesthetic innovation. He simply looked for artefacts that had the same blunt, meaningless, sensational impact, the same complete bankruptcy of political, aesthetic, poetic or ethical content as advertising imagery and declared its worth by setting a price on it. Having done that he could enhance and reinforce that worth by creating a scarcity or placing it in prestigious situations (the walls of the Tate Gallery for instance) that steeply enhanced its value. Some of his purchases were of works of established creative potency; paintings by Freud, Weight, Kossov, Auerbach and Kitaj. It was not impossible for a compulsive spendthrift to acquire contemporary work in which original information was still to be found. There were recent works by Victor Willing, by Alvis Neuman and Bill Woodrow. But his special significance in the cultural field became manifest when he turned to the unfortunate Julian Schnabel, a painter represented by Doris's friend Mary Boone, and bought a vast quantity of this unknown and deeply mediocre artist's work. Thus, at a stroke, he cast the previous long-standing dislocation between monetary and aesthetic values into obscurity. Schnabel, like Warhol's production team, could set no aesthetic value on his work to compete with the monetary value the purchaser established by bulk-buying. He had an ad-man's gimmick at that time of painting figurative pictures of people on canvasses covered with broken crockery. In these works the painted image destroyed the inherent *objét trouvé* qualities of the broken crockery, whilst the jagged edges and deep overlapping fissures failed to obscure the inept, evening-institute-art-class workmanship of the drawing and painting. Since then Schnabel has tried to further conceal his ineptitude behind Art Brut pastiches, all the while attempting a sad perpetuation of the artist-as-disaffiliated-hipster persona previously established in the era of Jackson Pollock, Jack Kerouac, Neal Cassady and the young Marlon Brando. Yet another dauber who would rather have been Elvis Presley.

In New York Robert Hughes had already spotted his worthlessness. In Britain Peter Fuller sprang to the attack: 'He is a painter with the imagination of a retarded adolescent,' Fuller wrote in Art Monthly, reviewing Schnabel's 1982 show at the Tate. 'No technical mastery,' he went on, 'no intuitive feeling for pictorial space; no sensitivity towards, or grasp of tradition: and a colour sense rather less developed than that of Congo the chimpanzee.' Practically the entire Schnabel exhibition at the Tate had been loaned by Charles and Doris Saatchi from their New York purchases. This loan demonstrated an almost invisible but ever present cunning on the part of the collectors. Mary Boone had made use of Saatchi's advice on marketing Schnabel in New York. She sold practically the entire show before it opened so that the outcry against the mediocrity of the canvasses could be silenced by the names of prestigious purchasers displayed alongside them. She could also deploy the Saatchi policy of using the public display, not to sell to the public but to establish the market worth at which this artist entered the arena, side-stepping evaluation placed upon it by critics, other artists and anyone able to discern facts. The language in which Boone announced herself and Schnabel as the 'first and foremost art stars of the decade' was purely and unabashedly the language of Rock and Roll hype.

Charles Saatchi was an habitual bulk buyer. He was aware that the purchase of an artist's work in quantity and his ostentatious expenditure on it would already promote it in the public's understanding of quality. To display it in Britain's national gallery of modern art would immediately give historic importance to the work, a qualification bestowed upon it by those appointed to make these decisions by Her Majesty's Government, which at that time had only recently come under the baton of the tyrannical adventuress Thatcher. The expert responsible in 1982 was Alan Bowness. For Charles Saatchi to have his own name alongside the work would have a subtle effect for both himself and Schnabel. His expenditure (the size of the bet) and Bowness's approval would promote this significantly dire work. The seemingly daring expenditure on work with a good deal of the eye-catching stunt about it would introduce the name of Saatchi to the world of art administration where he and his money would be welcomed and given a chair, in fact given several on several committees. As Waldemar Januszczak said: 'You could hardly move in the art world without bumping into the middle-man, usually Charles Saatchi. This was the year when the sweet stench of money returned to our galleries.'

Peter Fuller reacted rather differently: 'The Saatchis spend their time promoting a dominant cultural form i.e. advertising, which allows no space for the social expression of individual subjectivity. It is therefore predictable that they prefer fine art forms which are nothing but a solipsistic, infantile wallowing in the excremental gold of the otherwise excluded subjective dimension. Schnabel and Waddington are entitled, if they so wish, to serve the tasteless sensibilities of the advertising tycoon. But it is one thing for such people to pursue their degraded tastes in private and quite another for our leading modern art institution, the Tate Gallery, to indulge these tastes in public. I believe that Alan Bowness should indicate to us what the true aesthetic qualities of the Schnabels he has so freely purchased are: and if he cannot do so he should resign.'

It took a spin-doctor to know that he couldn't, he wouldn't and nobody cared, because it is a spin-doctor's business to know how shallow public understanding is, even in very high places, and how much people will spend in areas of previous profundity in order to terminate profundity and remain shallow.

Following the display of Schnabel and the buying and selling thereof, Bowness formed his Patrons of New Art, partly as a way of giving himself a supportive body that shared Charles and Doris Saatchi's preferences (which Saatchi further underlined at the time by praising *Dallas*, *Star Wars*, *ET* and the Marlboro ads and decrying *Jewel In The Crown* and *Brideshead Revisited*). Patrons of New Art was a body that could scrub round Friends of the Tate, who were beginning to grouse about the slack stuff coming into favour. The Duveen Gallery was retitled the Gallery of New Art and a New Art

Jury was appointed to decide what went into it. Prominent on the jury was Nicholas Serrota, at that time director of the Whitechapel Gallery. Out of these strategies the Turner Prize was created, originally to be called the New Art Prize. One can only conjecture who it was that thought to honour this annual contest of half-baked gesturalists with the name of one of the finest operators in the business of original information that ever lived. Charles Saatchi resigned from the Patrons Of New Art as a protest at having been accused of showing his Schnabels at the Tate to increase their value. Saatchi loves to absent himself. He scarcely ever attends his own private views.

In any case the damage was done. His hegemony was all but secure. He sold his Schnabels having made good use of them; buying in bulk, introducing himself, then selling in bulk. In Jonathan Glancy's words he had become 'in the hot house of modern art . . . a one man Stock Exchange; no-one dealing on his floor has much of a chance.' Thus he could continue his usual professional practice of getting and staying very rich. Later he shed his Hirsts, not quite at the price he hoped for, and guided by the inept Januszczak and a young self-styled painter called Martin Moloney, stocked up on the New Neurotic Realism. Thus he continues to maintain his unwarranted control.

But Saatchi's achievement lay beyond marketing. His effective political purpose was to establish what capitalism has increasingly held to be the only scale of value that had any authentic worth, that of money, into the very heart of non-monetary values. He, together with his political client, could construct an organisation of art that would occupy the space where art should be, with work that had no regenerative art potency and carried no threat whatever to the smooth running of monetary power groups. Thus real art would lose media coverage, lose media focus and would be cast into the shadows of a safe obscurity.

2.   FORGOTTEN MODELS

> (of Julian Schnabel) The cackhandedness is not feigned but real.
>
> Robert Hughes.

For a while the Turner Prize flickered. The professional sensationalism that presented the pregnant man on the Health Education Council posters and the words-unnecessary Silk Cut ads was applied in making the selection and certainly in attracted media attention. At the same time it attracted the same dismissive philistinism that had been directed to masterworks by Henry Moore and Graham

Sutherland in the past, a deadening British provincial indifference that is, somehow, quite different from the healthy energy of outrage.

And in the early stage there was still some art about. The first 1984 prize-winner, Malcolm Morley was a capable painter and had a raw tasteless comic-book vigour about him that gave him claims that the narcissistic Schnabel lacked even if he was (surprise surprise) also represented by Doris Saatchi's pal Mary Boone.

The next prize went to Howard Hodgkin who at one time had the uncanny ability to give the juicy paint-forms in his conversation pieces an uncanny cartoonist's likeness to the people represented. Even if, by 1985, he had regressed to such a formless degree that he might seem ideal for the necessary worthlessness of a Turner Prize-winner, he was well known to be the opposite of a philistine: a painter with a long-standing reputation, a collector of Persian miniatures, with no aspiration whatever to Rock and Roll stardom.

Gilbert and George in 1986 were more the sort of thing Saatchi was after. Commencing their careers with rather limp performance art, they had proceeded to the presentation of huge pieces in which photo-images of themselves were juxtaposed with photo-images of gross obscenity, shit, genital flesh, decay and racist graffiti, all in primary colours with the heavy black outline of stained glass giving them a kitsch sacredness. Roger Scruton spotted them. In *Modern Painters* he said 'Gilbert and George are certainly gifted and if their gifts appeal to such as Charles Saatchi then it is because they are practising the same trade as their patron. It would be wrong to say they were original. Andy Warhol showed the way.' More recently they returned to their performance mode affecting a robotic snapping of cameras at the funeral of Joshua Compston who ran the Factual Nonsense Gallery and choked on his own vomit after visiting the Jean-Michel Basquiat exhibition. The display was neither death nor art. It was affectlessness.

Richard Deacon in 1987 was an artist, not a very good one, but an artist more or less in the tradition of David Smith. Tony Cragg in '88 assembled arbitrary fragments into compositions redolent of the basic design exercises done on foundation courses in the late '50s. Richard Long, the land artist, followed in '89. His work, whilst not entirely touching the quick of inspiration, was certainly no empty market currency.

In 1990 there was no Turner Prize and it seemed briefly as if the strategies of Mammon had failed. Meanwhile things were happening at Goldsmith's College of Art under Michael Craig-Martin. An inflated mode of Post-Modernist gesturalism was under production, which manifested itself in three exhibitions called Freeze in an East End warehouse.

Here was art as vacuous as that of Schnabel, art precisely in the Rock and Roll, post-Warhol line of semi-literate mediocrity. For these young contenders had achieved, either deliberately or by coincidence, the synchronisation of Derrida's dismantling of history with the Rock Dome's determination to disregard the world-before-Elvis. This was art that saw vision, skills, genius, beauty, wit, anger, love, innovation, original information, art in fact, as a grand narrative bereft of credibility. It was vital to display, not art, but products totally devoid of the qualities that define art and its function. It would be charitable to think that this was an informed manifestation in line with the anti-art of Dada and Fluxus but a quick look at the egocentric polemic of these practitioners betrays such crusading hubris that any hope for an art which is consciously a 'representation of its own self-negation' (Derrida) is itself negated.

Away from the flock. Damien Hirst.

The Turner Prize recommenced in 1991 having found its tidal wave of hype.

Before a detailed analysis of the worthlessness of the non-artists competing for, and winning, the Turner Prize in the Nineties, it's beneficial to look at artists working in an earlier development of assemblage, *objéts trouvés* and installation, in Dusseldorf and Vienna. Here there was already a difficulty. Although cosseted and patronised by the wealthy and hip young tycoons of the German economic miracle, a significant number of these artists aligned themselves with the Marxist students assembled behind Rudi Dutschke and Danny Cohn-Bendit against the powers of Mammon on the west side of the Iron Curtain, and against the powers of Stalinism on the east. They thrived in the cleft stick of the Duchamp paradox, making their subversive jokes and their scenarios of outrage, yet selling them at *haut-couture* prices. One of them, Joseph Beuys, moved from delicate and compelling drawing and sculpture to the politics of a self-appointed messianic star, walking the streets of Belfast and other stricken cities with a demeanour not a million miles away from that of Michael Jackson's earthsong performance. His Coyote video, in which he stalks New York, lent pop video the trilby and fishing waistcoat image. Klaus Rinke's events with fire-hoses were immediate insignia of his alignment with

the Berlin students who were struggling into identical power-jets in their street battles with the police.

Robert Filiou, Ben Vautier, Robin Page all committed themselves to actions, gestures and even practical jokes (for instance, advertising an evening of their aggressive events as a 'programme of new music'). All carried out their art in the evasive and subversive vocabulary of true Dadaists and even true Situationists, seeking to erode and subvert the structures of capitalism by casting art into a language of action and biodegradable material which was hardly amenable to the market, being often literally untransportable, unstoreable and lacking any possibility of permanence. Yet simultaneously, they were happy to be acknowledged as artists by the then thriving Cologne and Dusseldorf art markets which, with all the extensive subtlety and skill for turning revolt into currency that capitalism has sustained in the late Twentieth Century, managed somehow to market their acts (sketches, notes, blueprints for, photographs of) and their junk. The difference between the artists of Fluxus and the contenders for the Turner Prize is that, while happy to take the bucks that came their way, they retained an identity separate from the market they milked, delivering their high-priced pieces of scribble and bric-a-brac and carrying out their tasks of dogged outrage with a crazy and aggressive contempt for the very public to which they were addressed.

Yves Klein was quite happy to take his patron's bundle of notes and throw them in the Seine, proclaiming calmly, when asked for the art work which the patron hoped to purchase, that the very act of flinging away the money was the art work. Klein's work certainly belonged to the art which comments on art rather than practises it. Nonetheless, although it exchanged the fact of aesthetics for the ambiguities of debate, it made the point with sadistic precision that what artists make is not what money buys. Intelligent patrons at this time recognised the need for such individuals as the robber barons recognised the need for clergy. Someone, they believed, should dwell outside the ramparts of market pressures and be paid to do so. Society, as its monetary core grew more centripetal, needed its sacred psychotics. Nam June Paik attended first nights with a knife to surreptitiously hack off saleable pieces of expensive Paris gowns in the foyer. Vautier commenced an event by hitting everyone in the front row in the face until someone stopped him. No-one hit back.

The Vienna Institute of Direct Art was more successful in placing art beyond the reach of marketability. Otto Muehl, Gunter Brus and Herman Nitsch mounted large scale sculpture ceremonies in which blood, pain, meat and sometimes death were used as materials. The much touted bisected cow of Damien Hirst dims a little in its shock impact, as do the Benetton snaps of birth and death, when compared with Nitsch disembowelling suspended steers in Viennese galleries, slithering viscera down onto powdered shoulders and smart Italian suits, rolling naked volunteers in swamps of guts, shit and food. Displays of self-laceration, defecation and copulation, in one case with a dildo fastened to the bleeding stump of a headless chicken, cast the artists into

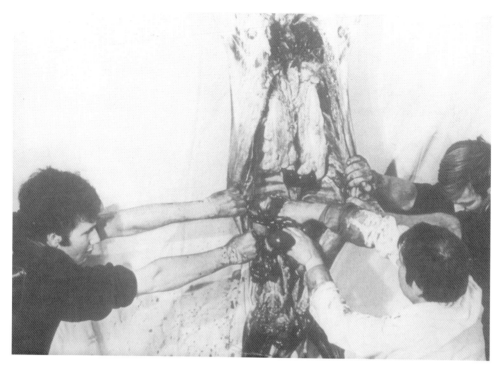

Henman Nitsch. Action Munich 1968.

jail repeatedly where they could scarcely be said to be the dupes of the all-pervading market. Capitalism resorted to containment of a simpler and more old fashioned kind in this case.

The Viennese events were certainly art, rising out of the brute primitivism of the Cobra painting group, revelling in the slithering stinking qualities of the flesh and its fluids. They were action and space structures with a keen eye to surface, colour, confinement and release,which partook of the urgency of shamanistic rituals, of Hindu laceration and Voodoo sacrifice. They claimed for art, in the hour of nuclear suicide, in a city on the separating line of the duellists, the right to employ trauma, not to command attention, much less to sell, and certainly not to deal in a devalued lexicon of qualities rendered meaningless by the post-modernist emasculation of meaning, but to alter human consciousness into a play with reality unprotected by taboo. They demonstrated the whole and necessary visceral panoply of life on earth which was threatened, a Dionysiac *sparagmos*.

When confronted with the work of the Turner contestants and the Saatchi purchases one is certainly struck with the fact that this work is less audacious than the work of Fluxus. The bric-a-brac of contemporary life is used without any close relationship between the artists and the object. The fishing jacket, the plasma and the lard were vital to Beuys when he was still a sculptor because their quality and their density touched in him a magically erotic evocation of survival. Beuys' work, like so much of the Fluxus work and the Viennese work, had its roots in the World War II experience, particularly the German defeat at Stalingrad, where war spawned its own fetishes in the minds of those enduring the slaughter. Compared with this Tracey Emin's project of displaying the ephemera of her life in an ongoing exhibition is flatly non-selective. To say, as a defender well might, that Emin's survival as a woman in the inner city of the Nineties is equivalent to surviving in the Siege of Stalingrad, is precisely the kind of self-evident nonsense that underlines Tracey's predicament. She is blinded to the wider agenda needed for proper evaluation of her work's significance, or lack of it, by the Rock and Roll Dome. World War II and, indeed, all taxing aesthetics, are pre-Elvis. Within the Dome if we want martyrdom, and, in a victim culture, it's often urgent for us to find it, our martyrdom must be protected from comparison with art springing from consequential horror, even though there's still a lot about. We tend to keep Rwanda and Bosnia outside the Rock and Roll Dome, grieving over the bruising we sustain from our onanistic pleasure-seeking and occasionally chucking a buck or two to the butchered.

We would also rightly note that the *audacity* of Fluxus and Vienna was far greater than that of a pickled sheep or a plastercast pisshole in the snow. The sheer chuckaway pokerface shrug of Vautier and Robin Page with their clanking shovels, their brick suppers, their abrupt unapologetic actual violence, compares revealingly with the way in which Rachel Whiteread and Damien Hirst present their material, gestures in no way flung by damaged aliens, but boxed up or cast and displayed nicely by the same firms that do the same jobs for trade fairs and theme parks, their packing cases and display tanks chosen from catalogue patterns whose language casts upon their audacity an air of belonging to the world at which the insult might once have been flung. Like Rock, we may still attempt credibility as tortured outsiders but the gear must be seen to be state-of-the-market. No point in hacking up your forearms for tenth rate photographic equipment. Suicides must only be promised through the best loudspeakers. We must shriek, sneer, bleed and occasionally very publicly die, but we must always be wealthy and, with ostentatious casualness, we must be smart. The display case is designed to define and display the product and the product, whether it be a new Peugeot, an Italian shoe or a sensational shock object, and declare that it is for sale. Art, with Saatchi, has paid the price of dropping all hope of having an identity-outside-the-market, for which Dusseldorf artists were paid.

3. NUMB DOWN

> Their titles are lifted from the gutter – 'two cocks',
> 'tongue fuck cocks', 'friendship pissing', 'shit faith'
> and the like – while the images fail to be disgusting only
> because Gilbert and George are so devoid of artistic
> talent as to be capable of producing no emotion whatsoever.
>   Roger Scruton.

In the market of transgression a disarming infantilism has come to prevail. When Vienna was shitting, disembowelling and buggering all over the arena there was the towering edifice of Judeo-Christian taboo to blow to pieces. The artists took on their own shoulders the repression of centuries which the world, in the early Sixties, still suffered. It quite simply seemed that one of the reasons for which the species was about to destroy itself might have been fear of the hidden detail of its existence. Shoving the intolerable into the open might have re-ignited human self-regard. By the Nineties, onanistic sex, facilitated by the birth control pill, accessible abortion and legalised homosexuality, had lifted sexual taboo completely, quickly detonating the puritanical anti-heterosexual backlash of Dworkin and McKinnon whose vocabulary, whilst condemnatory, is gauchely overt. Dworkin writes about sex in her novel *Ice and Fire*: 'She is lean and tough. She fucks like a gang of boys . . . She fucks everyone eventually with perfect simplicity and grace. She is a rough fuck. She grinds her hips in. She pushes her fingers in. She tears around inside. She is all muscle and jagged bones. She thrusts her hips so hard you can't remember who she is or how many of her there are. The first time she tore me apart. I bled and bled.' The pulp-fiction rhythm of the prose echoes the loveless act she describes. The bald crudity of the language is a calculated display in her onslaught on even the possibility of genital love. No compassion. No moral concern. Just a world-weary sado-masochist who hates her condition and must, in her world, sublimate her hatred in the form of a professional crusade. Jake and Dinos Chapman with their compound figures with multiple attached willies and fannies, the much talked-about, strangely inflated wee-wee splashing of Andres Serrano (Piss Christ) and Helen Chadwick (Piss Flowers), the stunningly displayed shit pictures of Gilbert and George, Jeff Koons' shift from kitsch to pornography with his unsparingly lit close-ups of his prick up his wife's arse, Mona Hatoum's cinematic tour of her vaginal passage, even Mapplethorp's tellingly elegant snaps of rough trade with its elephantine dick out, all have an aura of infantile compulsive anal and genital play which may be inevitable when sex is left foundering behind, having been stripped of its dignifying connotations of love and reproduction. In a situation where the understanding of penile penetration as being a sacred ceremony of adoration ('With my body I thee worship') sparks angry outrage, in exactly the same way that the word 'fuck' once did, outrage becomes difficult.

Artists make a display of their cool detachment from their genitalia but display their detachment to detonate the hot impact of an explosive gimmick. Punk did similar things better twenty (not ten, not fifteen, but twenty) years ago. In the hands of people who are only outraged by a threat to their assumed right to self-appeasement, outrage has had most, if not all, of its teeth drawn.

Outrage in art needs anger and anger needs love, the kind of anguished, yearning, caring, irresolvable involvement with others that has long ago been castigated under the Rock and Roll Dome. The late novelist, Kathy Acker, then teaching in San Francisco, managed to completely depersonalise her orgasms by deriving them from the vibrations of vulvic rings.

And one would be right to be astonished at the ignorance of the Turner contestants. There might occasionally be a practitioner who has distinguished himself in the dense thicket of Structuralist and Post-Modernist thought but there are few who know the work with which their star performances must be compared. They should know that Schwitters, Picasso and Marcel Duchamp worked with found objects, selected them better, and placed them with greater wit and greater effect. They should know that Dada and Fluxus broke more taboos with greater courage and more attack. They should know that Schwitters, Rosenquist, Thiebaud, Lichtenstein, Paolozzi, Peter Philips, Jim Dine, Red Grooms, Mel Ramos, Richard Hamilton, Larry Rivers, Ed Keinholz and Bruce Lacey, all manipulated the imagery of the popular culture with sharper observation and a wider awareness of the qualities inherent in their material. And, mysteriously, they don't.

This is partly because they deeply resent that anyone old enough to remember pre-Presley standards and the pre-Presley world should come near them. Under the Rock and Roll Dome of bland egalitarianism and suspended comparisons, when stardom is a political mandate for all who want it (at least as basic a human right as a computer, a state-of-the-technology sound-deck and a promiscuous sex-life), comparisons are bound to be disdained, not because they are true or untrue. Truth and the lack of it are, after all, uncertain entities. Neither are they to be disdained because they are out-of-date, belonging to an antiquated standard of assessment. They are to be disdained because it is tacitly and confidentially believed that the world was made over, begun again with Elvis, and that any information from outside this fresh start is an obstruction to those who have to live it out. Under the information system of electronic filing and communication, of the media, and of capitalist consumer culture, a difficult if limited game must be played. Other information is outside the agenda.

For finally, after all these comparisons, the conclusion must be that the touted young art stars of the Millennium are not worse nor better than their close equivalents in the past. They are different, doing a different job, involved in a different profession. They cannot be artists under the Rock and Roll Dome because under that reduced impenetrable shell, art no longer exists. That's the way Warhol wanted it and

Jake and Dino Chapman. Zygatis accelleration etc, etc.
... an aura of infantile compulsive anal and genital play ...

Gilbert and George. Spunk and Tears.

Helen Chadwick. Piss Flower.
... wee-wee splashing ...

Saatchi wants it. Art is the leak in, and the corrective to, all power structures. In the triumph of capitalism under the Rock and Roll Dome the enemy, if he survives at all, must be rendered invisible.

4.   DUMB

> The notion that this man (Julian Schnabel) is an
> emanation of the zeitgeist matches his fantasies
> about himself. It even had a small truth, since only a
> culture as sodden with hype as America in the
> early 80's could have underwritten his success.
> Robert Hughes.

Mark Wallinger, whose tedious paintings of horses might be touted by defenders of the Turner Prize as evidence of surviving depictive skill, reveals why his handling of paint is less remarkable than that of any jobbing hack in a commercial studio when he talks about Cézanne. As Kathy Acker's sexual spectrum is much reduced so is Wallinger's appreciation of what painters have ever been doing. 'Painting,' says Wallinger is not the result of an artist's individual endeavour but 'is a product of popular culture.' No it isn't. The popular culture of Cézanne's time was Punch, Harpers, Marie Lloyd, Caran D'Ache, Gilbert and Sullivan and La Goulu, none of whom are distinguishable in Mont Saint Victoire. And popular culture, says Wallinger, began with Daguére and Fox Talbot. No it didn't. Popular culture is as old as folklore. Photography was an eccentric gentleman's science, about as popular as archaeology, Egyptology and mesmerism. Late in the same piece the jargon starts to emerge which betrays Wallinger's stupefying cocoon of Post-Modernist dogma. Cézanne's work was an 'interrogation of subjectivity'. Cézanne's early paintings, says Wallinger, were 'free of any discernible talent'. Wallinger is certainly free of any talent for discernment which is possibly why his own work is free of any quality except a sort of meretricious schoolboy gift.

'Cubism,' Wallinger goes on to say, 'was the dullest movement of all', only valued by 'formal determinism' which leads to formalism's 'tautological apogee: paint as paint'. Well, paint has been paint for some time, each artist finding it necessary to diminish the descriptive function of the work in order to make available the sensory delights of the substance, from the tactile pastes of Titian's nudes, through the near-edible toasted crusts of Rembrandt to the colour-floods of Matisse and the shudder skids of Francis Bacon. Any artist who finds Cubism dull is, probably to his

Mark Wallinger. Half Brother (Denis Keen)

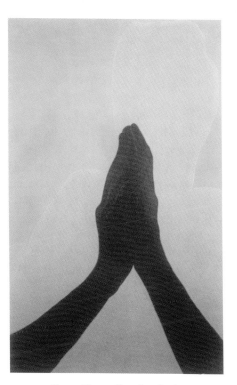

Garry Hume. Begging for it.
... they're just paintings...

Neil Jenney. Hunter and Hunted.
... mock expressive brush-strokes ...
irony for ineptitude ...

considerable relief, clearly as immune to the dilemma of initial information as a man in a coffin is immune to the wind and the rain.

Finally in the same statement, Wallinger confesses that the century needs witnesses rather than artists. In that case Wallinger should get in the dock (or at any rate the loose-box) with his garbled narratives.

Tracey Emin, also reacting to Cézanne, calls his quivering evocation of hot Provence "pastel colours" revealing that her only previous reference point for colour was the decorator's chart. She is not, she says, 'interested in Cézanne, or that period of French painting. It is,' she says, 'male, boring and bourgeois.' That would be why Manet's *Olympia* caused fights in the gallery and all the Impressionists, including Berthe Morrisot and Marie Cassat (most of whom lived in dire poverty) were slung out of the Salon year in, year out. It was during this time that 'bourgeois' became a French artist's strongest term of condemnation.

Anthony Gormley, who reproduced in clay a horde of creatures not unlike the 'shmoos' invented by cartoonist Al Capp fifty years ago, finds Cézanne's significance lies in being one of the ancestors of video artists like Gary Hill and Bill Viola which is a little like saying that Wagner must have had something going for him because he influenced Lloyd-Webber, or that Epstein's *Lucifer* finds validity by heralding Gormley's Angel of the North.

The Guardian newspaper, which wrung these *bon mots* concerning Cézanne from Wallinger, Emin and Gormley, does us all a service by giving a number of Saatchi's surrogates a small platform in the 'Brush With Genius' column. Keith Coventry, talking about Neil Jenney's dire painting *Hunter and Hunted*, applauds the work's 'mock expressive brushstrokes'. Claiming irony for ineptitude is here making a virtue of necessity, rather like the tone-deaf Sid Vicious pretending to guy the high talent of Sinatra's *My Way*. 'What's the best way to present my idea? – Make a painting. What colour is the sky? – Blue. What colour is the grass? – Green. The result is "bad" painting, very post-modern.' A young and wealthy Saatchi surrogate praises another surrogate for the direct and simple way he eschews art. That total certainty that exists when maker and means fuse into an uninvited fact of threatening consequence is as professionally denied as real sex was denied by Acker's twinkling twat.

Hadrian Piggot waxes enthusiastic about Bertrand Lavier's *Ronis No. 2*, a steel locker covered with impasto which refers back to Jasper Johns, Jim Dine, Rauschenberg and Duchamp, by comparison with whom it stands revealed as the limp late event it is. What is revealed is Piggot's contentment in a kind of playdough innocence that would be threatened by any such devaluing comparisons. He likes it because for him it shines a new light on Artex. There is no way one can sense about the '96 Turner contestants, Simon Peterson, Douglas Gordon and Gary Hume, that they recognise the sheer emptiness of their work. Nor is there the Jack-The-Lad audacity of even Damien Hirst. Their public demeanour, as studied as that of a rock star sprawled across the couch on a chat show, is one of ennui. Patterson takes familiar formats, such as an underground tube map or a set of wind sails, and replaces the words you might expect with arbitrary names. The sails are writers. The tube stations are anybody. There are, after all, rather a lot of them for the names to have anything in common. Takes research, that. Douglas Gordon shows films slowly. Gary Hume paints anything anyhow insofar as he is able to, lacking manual ability. 'People say my drawing is terrible,' he says to the man from the Independent 'but it's the best I can do. They're just paintings,' he says. 'It's wet stuff on the end of a stick with my hand attached.' Such figures are drones in the art-hive, richly rewarded with money and fame for making sure that they do next to zero and they disengage themselves from what may have been considerable intelligence. They are bored, but they are not stretched. And they are cool. Showing with them is an artist called Cragie Horsfield. He makes fine solemn photographs with the skill, dedication and concern the other contenders so rigorously avoid. The photographs depict facts. Horsfield's feeling for what they depict is a fact and the accuracy he brings to his presentation is a fact. The others must be a bit embarrassed. Horsfield refers back to Bill Brandt, Bert Hardy and Dorothea Lang. It is important under the Rock and Roll Dome to burn any evidence that other cultures were in any way superior. In such a jealously protected play-space it is a relief to disdain any need for thought beyond that which a computer can encompass, and to hand over the keyboard to a financier who pays big money to those happy to stay gaga. During the prestigious Sensation exhibition at The Royal Academy in 1997 the public and even the art world, began to register an informal disgust for the exhibits. Newly embraced artists who had been admitted to the previously exclusively traditional halls of the Academy resigned and an overall mediocrity was noted. Emin compensated by appearing endearingly drunk on TV.

PART SEVEN

Maggie

Benetton showed its colours recently by opening a store
in Sarajevo just a few hundred yards from the food market
where 41 people were killed by artillery fire in August –
Sarajevo developed a relationship with the Benetton name
after photographer Oliver Toscani produced an ad-image
of the bloody uniform of a Bosnian soldier that became a
rousing poster for the resistance plastered throughout the
city. In addition to Benetton ware the boutique sports
seven-foot-high cement barricades in front of the shop
windows to protect shoppers from flying shrapnel.

W (women's-wear glossy)

1. THE BIG PRODUCTION

Guy Debord, the artist who took the hard political edge of Surrealism, honed it into a discipline called Situationism, saw it fail, then faded into booze, focused much on what he called 'spectacle'.

He referred to the spectacle which the establishment deploys to stupefy the people. This was clearly the insight of a man raised under Roman Catholicism, a man aware that the very faith condemning the graven image invented the crucifix, the most commonplace of the lot, a colossal ikon of perpetual emotional blackmail spanning two millennia of detailed oppression. The pomp and ceremony of kings and clergy, the military tattoo and the civic parade, all were spectacle. And so, Debord accurately spotted, were the media – the television, the blockbuster movie, the front page, the catwalk and the rock festival. He even went further and argued that art itself had become a corrupt obstacle to human freedom.When the artist militates against his own potency, victory is granted to the exploiter, the commercial stupifier whose opponent, the artist, has disarmed himself.

The question concerns the existential dilemma in which the image was situated. If it was a device designed by and for a self-perpetuating oppressive establishment, a controlling praxis, it was indeed the 'spectacle' that concerns DeBord. If it arose spontaneously within a culture, in order to propel that culture into an extended future it was the self-perpetuating social gene that Richard Dawkins calls a meme, part of a process which, in a rigorous Darwinian understanding, is apolitical and amoral. If it was a gift by which an individual helped his fellow creatures to enjoy experiences which he was uniquely able to give, then it was art. And if the language produced rather than expressed the society that used it, it was Structuralist text, semiology, part of an unfolding process to which we shall all eventually be exposed whether the artist donates it to us or not. The problem we had to deal with repeatedly was to do with the fact that, whichever our image may be among the above varieties, it frequently looked exactly the same as images belonging to other categories. The need was to determine how, in the resulting confusion, the proven power of such ikons had fallen into the hands of abusive, exploitative or oppressive agents.

We have examined how Andy, rock, drugs, post-modern ignorance and advertising, between them all contributed to the fusion and confusion of charged images, and how one of the first politicians to take advantage of this wealth of powerful imagery, which could be so easily abused, was Margaret Thatcher. The spectacle against which Debord railed was indeed extended to encompass the art spectacle that his predecessors, the Surrealists, had once fired at the establishment like poisoned canisters in some psychological germ warfare. In the early Seventies politics was still half-sunk in the patrician convention of the old governing class. A party that did not claim its power on a basis of honest verbal debate would fear dismissal as trivial, vulgar and opportunist. Maggie didn't care too much to hang about with this dusty sense of Oxbridge decorum. The ad-men were spinning the world and she wanted to join them. She was the first British politician to employ an expert spectacle manipulator. She let Saatchi and Saatchi change her and she let them advise her. In time the Labour Party under Tony Blair would have to ditch everything it supposedly stood for in order to play her game and topple the Government she initiated. Their Saatchi was Peter Mandelson.

First she had to be told that her own perfect embodiment of the genteel garden party stereotype was perpetuating a class war whose simplistic alignments energised her enemies. Saatchi and Saatchi recognised the power of Britain's ancient feudal class divisions and proceeded to juggle with its imagery. They chose Elsie Tanner, one of the most popular *Coronation Street* regulars, as possibly the most loved character in the British media gallery, a mature woman of sadness, dignity and earthy power, fusing the merits of the undefeatable individual with those of the neighbourhood matriarch and the golden-hearted tart. Elsie's hair was styled into a huge defiant frontal wing that paid reference to the sexy bangs of Forties film stars like Ava Gardner and Rita Hayworth, and also to the windswept headgear of pirates, cowboys, Ghurkas and Anzacs. Elsie was raunchy, powerful and sane. With a little of her image, her hairdo anyway, Maggie would lose her repellent embodiment of the headmistress everybody wanted to decapitate.

It took the Saatchi organisation to know that amongst what Thatcher and the Conservative Party considered their opposition, the Trades Unions and Wilson's expanded universities, the battered legions of Scargill and Cohn-Bendit, the working class and the more visible citizens of the Rock and Roll Dome, various anomalies had sprouted which a reconstructed Tory could exploit. Within the working class there was even greater latent reaction against drugs and dissipation than there was among the landed gentry where eldest sons had been lounging in the orangerie with spikes and velveteen loons for some time now. Nationwide there was a profound nostalgia for the binary options of the Second World War – comfortable goody and baddy, master and servant roles, clarified by the lines of battle and military rank, a binding common ethic of a national crusade against an obviously evil enemy. It was clear who was the affection figure in *Til Death Do Us Part*. A significant number wanted good old songs that were designed for community singing in pub, NAAFI and shelter; uniforms, fashions and hairstyles that were ready to be reclaimed into an overstimulated culture that needed to plunder dead modes before the corpses were cold. Thus there was a connecting link with the new rock priesthood. As Thatcher came to cabinet, and punk, the last twitch of Rock and Roll carrying any credibility of cultural intercession, rumbled on the horizon, somewhere between David Bowie and Brian Ferry there came a reaction against the hippie movement. Allen Ginsberg and Emmet Grogan vanished as role models, only to be replaced by prototypes culled from Busby Berkeley, Fred Astaire and Jack Buchanan, while the costume of jazz, the gangster suit and the overhead-lit trilby, were transposed from the still-suspect jazz scene to the Rock and Roll platform. Anybody mounting a major event in the language of the Forties would reap tremendous response.

It was a short twenty years from the point where Spike Milligan and the Alberts had deployed the Union Jack as a ludicrous emblem of ridiculed patriotism, through its dissociated usability on Carnaby Street carrier bags, to its appearance in greasy impasto on the faces of West Ham supporters. Two commemorative festivals, one celebrating the Battle of Britain, the other the D-Day landings, all replete with jeeps, Spitfires, victory rolls, suspender belts, ATS bloomers and even Vera Lynn brought out of aspic to set us all singing again, these proved the hidden power of a hunger that only needed to be detonated by a perceptive manipulator.

In 1982 Margaret Thatcher's seat of power was perilous. The Elsie Tanner bang had gone some way to ingratiate her with the working class enterpreneurs who were to consolidate the Thatcher monetarist revolution of the Eighties, but it was still necessary to turn off the pub telly in Liverpool and Glasgow to save the set from flying glasses whenever her face appeared. Nests of virulent hatred still festered briskly. She needed a new weapon.

In the ambiguous cultural soup where the *objéts trouvés* of artists comingled with the logo, the icon, the advertising image and the role model, the Vietnam War had several times been suggested as a possible master 'happening' (ie action artwork) of the era. The psychiatrist Joseph Berke suggested it in a challenging piece of cultural analysis. Here was an army of freaks, their remaining brains saturated with deluding chemicals, supported by a massive grant from the Pentagon to create the biggest lightshow and continual fireworks display all of the time. Photographers Donald McCullum and Sean Flynn waxed lyrical about the war in terms of its excitement and transcendental glory. It was in the early Eighties that a massive piece of mural graffiti appeared in an underpass in drug-replete Hulme, Manchester – PRAY FOR WAR – under which some responding soul had written COOL SLOGAN. The blockbuster movies about the Vietnam War were yet to come – the *Deerhunter*, *The Killing Fields*, *Apocalypse Now*. They all contributed to this inane cosmeticisation of atrocity.

It has still not been revealed whether it was by collusion or coincidence that Argentina laid on the war that Maggie needed to close the ranks behind her. Opinions have been put forward, but not too loudly, that Galtieri's position was also perilous, that he too could have conceivably saved his political neck by promoting himself to the role of champion or martyr. This view is widely held in Argentina. NATO, the USA and her own Ministry of Defence were a real bore, trying to procure peace right up to the last minute. Thatcher characteristically dispatched her Defence

Minister, the humiliated William Pryor, to America for peace talks while she and the Saatchis got on with the movie.

It required an incisive and sceptical reading of imagery to discern that the style of the troop embarkation was a small masterpiece of Forties nostalgia, politically deployed. It had been some time since troops had been moved by boat. The reinvention of the troop-ship in Portsmouth Harbour, complete with tiers of grinning squaddies going to fight for a Britannia that looked as though she'd got her lion back, singing *Bless'Em All*, mixed in with *My Way* and *We Shall Overcome*, waving flags as young mums held up the toddler to wave back to brave daddy, equalled the disinterment of Vera Lynn. One still conjectures whether or not they were all switched over to waiting aircraft on the Isle of Sark.

This was not to be a war in the manner of Napalm-spraying helicopters, of push-button holocaust with Jim Morrison on the Walkman. This was a proper war, with paratroops, berets, rucksacks and bayonets. The media were censored of all negative images as rigorously as any Pathé Pictorial newsreels ever were. The British wounded, wracked, broken and bleeding, were delayed in their treatment, circling over obscure West Country airfields to keep them off camera. A certain crass disregard for the suffering of those members of society who the Premier believed to be an anachronism is just as vital to self-promotion in Rock and Roll politics as it is in drug-dealing or multi-national industry. The silly captain of the Belgrano had either wised up or just not read his shooting script. Anyway he had to be chased. Bang you're dead.

Just which details relating to this disgusting and elaborate production had been relayed to the Shrewsbury peace campaigner Hilda Murrell is unknown. A relative in the Admiralty had possibly leaked something to her. It is a mark of what a tough and resolute woman she must have been if it had become necessary to kill her to retrieve the information. It is a mark of the awful power the Saatchis had won for Thatcher that any protest against the idiotic verdict of 'death-by-ordinary-burglar' that was brought in by a Shrewsbury post-mortem was slight and quickly silenced.

Maggie continued in her new mode of government-by-media, sweeping her propaganda into television current affairs programmes and news presentations, imposing a censorship that practically forbade any opposition to her power, increasingly confident that the nation was, in fact, the Conservative Party and that all democratic opposition was traitorous. She defeated the Unions in 1985 with American advice. Possible sub-texts emerged in her public proclamations at this time, happily putting the SAS in police uniforms, having riot-trained strike-breakers from the Met flashing their bankrolls at the impoverished miners. America was clearly her favoured nation and the clapped-out society of culturally disenfranchised punters who had elected her was becoming an embarrassment. She proclaimed society to be non-existent, but she never actually revealed how well she knew that multi-national money, lubricated by computer technology, had made political debate redundant. Her sycophancy to the Americans was not based on Churchill's contentions about the

English-speaking world as much as it was based on her bestowal of all authority on wealth and the points from which wealth is generated. Her defeat of her own people, insofar as they were represented by the miners, was facilitated by Arthur Scargill's and Neil Kinnock's personal demeanour. Saatchis knew that it had become embarassing for your previously Labor-voting Rock and Roll Dome citizen to align himself with anyone so unfashionable, even by confidential ballot.Never mind closed-down hospitals and crumbling schools. What about those sideburns and that antiquated jiving to trad jazz?

Kinnock waves from the beach like any friendly bloke (always suspect in the world of personal space where friendliness is redefined as social harassment), trips over in the shingle, falls. In go the cameras like piranhas knowing that this image will win success in Maggie's Saatchi-trained image-circus where image is all, where that intelligent, ethical appraisal of content that felled the MacMillan government and the Nixon presidency is a thing of the past.

London. 1989.
'I'll just go and powder my nose,' says Claire. 'Now you boys be good.'

We sit in the shadowy candle-lit section of the Chelsea Arts Club. Claire had been flattered by Jay's attention – 'PR for Saatchi and Saatchi,' she says. 'I mean he's no chicken but he's bucks.'

The Chelsea Arts Club is a pre-rock oasis. It is in many ways the opposite alternative to the Groucho Club in the fatigued London of the Nineties. People go to the Groucho to be recognised. Rock and media celebrities go to the Chelsea Arts Club if they want to avoid recognition.

Jay wears his years well. There is no extra weight on him. He has a light tan. He orders a salad and drinks Perrier, leaving the wine to Claire and I.

'We are enemies, you and I,' he says as soon as Claire is out of earshot.

'Fucking right,' I say, 'but this is Claire's party so don't lets spoil it. There's just a couple of things I want to know before she gets back.'

'What are they?' he says.

'First Over The Wall,' I say 'whose idea was that?'

'Mine,' he says.

'And who designed the Falklands war?'

'I did.'

2.   THE SECRET ASSASSINATION OF BRITISH SOCIALISM

If Thatcher knew how to usurp the realm of floating imagery, Blair recognised that the route to success lay in the continuation of the monetarism Thatcher had established, and that his means to this success would have to be the fluidity of verbal definition that has sprung up through Structuralist jargon and computer-speak. If you can file and call it 'storing to memory', if you can transfer and call it 'downloading', if you can call the Dionysian 'abject', and revolution 'reconstruction', if you can call a slump a 'recession', then you can call consumer capitalism 'Labour'. Before this you must step into the Labour leadership at a time of crisis; Then you must rely on the tacit hope of Labour voters that your piece-by-piece abandonment of Socialism is an electioneering strategy to be mercifully rectified after the election. Finally you must convince the disillusioned new Tories, Dome-bred and nourished on fashion, image and 'attitude', that Labour, a mere word, is banner enough under which to continue the Thatcherite principles of brute careerism and greed.

'Attitude,' comes, beneath the Dome, to mean animation, rhetoric, hyperbole, hubris and gaga optimism, and is, of course, as empty as Blair's smile which is proving, as catastrophes accumulate on Indian frontiers, in French provincial town squares, in hospitals, schools and prisons, as irremovable as that of the late Reginald Bosanquet.

But emptiness is the Post-Modern mode. The void, rectangular spaces of the Saatchi Gallery, the slack, unlined, unpatterned and untextured fabric of the perpetually casual dress-style, the vapid nursery humour of successful sitcoms, the gap-headed infantilism of football fanatics, acid-house ravers, the rigid and dedicated refusal of all thought, passion, love, wit or honour is the first necessary element in the style of our time and Blair has found out how to embody it.

Thus, like Thatcher he will remain in power far longer than we can afford him, wreaking havoc merrily in all our quarters until we must face reality because fact will be all there is left to face, the fact of the blood on our own hands in Kosovo, the fact of Milosovic's victims dispersed permanently beyond their own frontiers, the fact of the Chinese nuclear arsenal, for fabrications will run dry under the Rock and Roll Dome and there is a great big nothing at all in the Millennium Dome to revive them.

PART EIGHT

WRECKAGE

The 1993 Venice Biennale marked a moment when the cult
of violence itself became a kind of formal aestheticism.
Adam Gopnik.

It opens a path for the viewer in areas of experience which
are not anti-moral or amoral but extra-moral. We take a
holiday from our ethics into a world created from death
and violence about which we are invited not to care – a
world where bad taste is driven to a point of elegance and
disgust filtered into delight.
Damien Hirst

As the self-proclaimed armies of liberation, people's
movements and fronts degencrate into marauding bands
indistinguishable from their opponents. The crazed
alphabet they hid behind, FLNA or FLNS, MPLA or FMLA,
cannot disguise the fact that no goal, no plan, no idea
binds them together other than the strategy (which hardly
merits the name) of plunder, death and destruction.
What gives today's civil wars a new and terrifying slant is
the fact that they are waged about *nothing at all*. That
gives them the characteristics of a political retrovirus.
Hans Magnus Enzensberger.

1.   KILLING JOKES

> We are seeing young and younger children
> committing more and more violence and murders –
> hideous crimes – They don't consider the
> consequence of their actions. To them a jacket or a
> pair of sneakers is as important as cash to a bank
> robber – They resent people who they think cause
> them misery and will kill for that.
>
> Professor Jack Levine.

London. 1994.
There are about half-a-dozen of them in the back of the bus. They wear immaculate school uniforms and carry briefcases. In the bus's gloom their waxy sepia cheeks reflect the street lamps along Hammersmith Bridge.
'So I fucking got him, this white boy, and he was fucking shitting himself 'cos he was lame, you know? So I tripped him up and then I fucking put the boot in. And he was crying, fucking crying, you know? No don't laugh, it was really good, you know?'
'What about that white boy with asthma. We brought on – You know? He was so scared! – We brought on his fucking asthma. His fucking mum had to take him away from the school he was so scared. We used to kick fucking shit out of him every fucking day.'
Their teeth gleam and their eyes weep in hilarity and excitement.
A woman says: 'I suppose you think that's clever then?'
'Hush,' says her husband. 'They've got guns.'

Cruelty has changed. It has become a recreational pastime of great levity and glee practised frequently by children. It has acquired grace and style and is very fashionable. Movies require it if they are to succeed and cruelty needs violent movies if it is to thrive in a culture of consensual tolerance. If we are to continue to enjoy that strange flight of total licence on football terraces, on cross channel boats, in Brixton pubs, in shopping centres, tube escalators and late-night buses we need to see young people selected for their handsome faces, their lithe nubile bodies, their grace and their lovingly designed, impeccably fashionable garments, and know that they casually cause in one another great spoutings of blood, great arterial pumpings, flayings, cleavings and shattering of the body's palace. The body must be elegant and it must be expendable. A bulky Edward G., a hang-dog Bogie, a bug-eyed Bette Davis, with their inimitable flaws and their weighty existential backdrag would not be welcome if they arrived in modern Hollywood. Film has largely ceased to be drama, and has become instead dance, not so much of dancers but of cantilevered, wheeled cameras moving around, as performers formalise and intensify their performance spaces by the implied but invisible trajectories of bullets, missiles, infra-red rays, sometimes even the bolts from crossbows.

This vocabulary started to manifest itself in the Sixties concurrently with the sophistication of Rock and Roll and the advent of sick humour.

Sick humour was a development of black humour, a favourite sweetmeat of the Surrealists and their also-rans. The height of black humour was the moment in Buuel's movie, *The Nazarene*, when the Jesus figure, entering the plague-stricken household, gently draws the sheet up to cover the face of the dead young wife only to reveal the corpse of a half-born child between her legs – a sour and bleak piece of low-key farce about the ineffectuality of human bids for decency and dignity in the face of death and mortality. It is a humour in which the savage exultancy is tempered with a wry regret and a complicit irony in the acknowledgement of a shared predicament. It is also ethically tempered by its existential character as a weapon against the damaging hypocrisy of church and bourgeoisie.

Black humour spread wildly from the delicate blasphemy of camp novelist Ronald Firbank to the angry and exultant erotic assaults on the clergy by Clovis Trouille, a self-taught painter much loved by the Surrealists, and the cartoonist Siné whose work caused a riot in the house of Penguin in the Mid-Sixties. The artists were clearly seen to be in a pointedly subversive role.

When sick humour developed out of black humour there were subtle differences in the language and the mode of presentation. Sick humour, in the prose of William Burroughs, on the lips of Lennie Bruce, was compulsive. There was an uncomfortable realisation that the artist had no economy to his rhetoric. Having made his point the sick humourist couldn't stop – he was obsessive, mesmerised by his material, compelled into a limitless litany of cruelty and nausea by a masturbatory sado-masochism that belied what subversive pretensions the work may have had. In the case of both Burroughs and Bruce, heroin was a big factor in the formation of their vision. Theirs was not an anger attacking helplessness. Theirs was the resignation of the addict, a transference of the helpless condition of addiction to the whole social arena. This resignation was a new note in art and it was not to diminish.

Violence coupled with black humour was the compelling mix that rendered the James Bond movies popular. Thronged with a rich parade of gross comic-book inventions like hook-handed hit men and overdrive divas, these ballets of car stunt, these sci-fi fantasies of gadgetry and escape focused on laugh shots like the car containing an unconscious man being compressed at the wrecker's allowing the camera to zoom in on the blood oozing from between the wrinkles of the cubed metal. Bond's indifference, his seamless unimpeded course through the laugh-timed holocausts, was a long way from the comic naivety of *The Nazarene* or the urbane heartlessness of characters such as the one played by Dennis Price in *Kind Heart and Coronets*. Here was an enviable erotic athlete who got away with everything, not even sweating or messing up his shirt, being far too preoccupied with a lithe progression from fantasy fuck to fantasy fuck to be impeded by compassion, morality or vulnerability. Confronted daily with the revolution in TV news coverage of war and horror in Vietnam, we needed a mode of distancing. Bond, the elegant psychopath, became a major role mode.

Simultaneously technology permitted a vertical advance in the special effects that had always been the anchor technique of the grand-guignol genre. Now eyeballs could slide loose and utterly realistic brains could follow them out of the socket. X-ray film made whole visceral skinless figures easy, whilst the accuracy of the portrayal of chancres and buboes made these horrors such common coinage that they became the collectable items of cult enthusiasts rather than the trauma that sent an audience reeling away to a life of pacifism and good works. Such enthusiasts were more apt to laugh and applaud as they shrieked than to weep or vomit. The horror genre at a comic level, as in the films of Russ Meyer, or at an art level in films like *The Exorcist* and *The Shining* multiplied its following. Such an audience was well insensitised against horror. The burning Buddhist on the Six O'Clock News would provoke challenges of make-up technique and lighting rather that politics and human shock. Among that audience were David Lynch and Quentin Tarantino.

Winter 1944. Dead German soldier.

Westerns developed a majestic elegance of violence in the Sixties. The lifting of sexual taboos, the cinematic trickery that enable the bowie knife to sever a pumping artery in wounds that vomited bright red appeared in Peckinpah, in the orgy of thinly disguised ludic sadism called *Soldier Blue*, eventually in the vast, measured fatalistic poems of cruelty-in-the-landscape by Serge Leone, with their twanging electro-rock-influenced sound-tracks of loss and desolation. Simultaneously the *Mad Max* films achieved moonscapes of butchery which the world was shortly to imitate.

The Moors Murderers were the first serial killers Britain had seen since Neville Heath twenty years previously. Following them, serial murder was to become commonplace culminating in the programmes of the Wests in their lodging house in Gloucester and the massacre of children in the school at Dunblane. Concurrently, serial killer movies became a genre, moving from the bizarre contrived horror of *The*

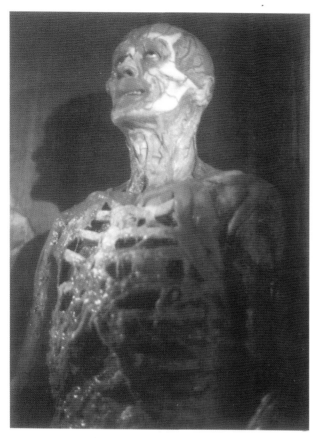

Bob Keen. Special FX from Hellraiser.

Silence of the Lambs through the utterly professional inner city social realism of the *Prime Suspect* series and *Cracker*, to the fake contention surrounding *Natural Born Killers*, largely enhanced by make-up departments increasingly adept at making flayed corpses and areas of grossly bruised flesh.

The end of *The Silence of the Lambs* is a piece of highly significant ethical bankruptcy when the escaped Hannibal Lecter telephones the investigator with whom he has by now formed a relationship of some mischievous warmth, making himself an impish affection figure, then puts down the phone to pursue the next object of his unspeakable appetites as the audience smiles slyly.

The way is paved and the scene set. Horror imagery has lost the nave comic vulgarity of the ghost train and the end-of-the-pier rubbermask shops, and has become sleekly realistic, not immediately distinguishable from the newsreel shots of the real thing. A confusion between science fiction and screen reportage follows immediately. Both are in any case a winking lozenge in the corner of the living room. The debate is endless concerning cross fertilisation between fictional screen, documentary screen, and day-to-day reality and conduct. It seems optimistic however to deny interfusions, as defenders of pornography and screen violence commonly do, when you read the following: 'Yesterday, just hours after the jailing of the Brookside Two, the campaign for their release was mobilised . . . Channel 4's switchboard was jammed with telephone messages from viewers outraged at the verdict, women's charities nation-wide were flooded with calls from battered women considering for the first time leaving their partners. And on the set of the Liverpool soap yesterday, Brookside creator Phil Redmond was tackling a demonstration by Women Against Domestic Violence, brandishing placards declaring Mandy's and Beth's innocence.' (Guardian 18/5/95)

If screen fiction and social reality are so enmeshed in the minds of a media-besotted public, the denial that screen psychopathy is unconnected to an increase in mindless viciousness in society is unsustainable. It has seldom been so clearly demonstrated that the notion (in this case involving two fictional characters) has become as provocative as the fact. Was it really a coincidence that Chucky the Doll in *Child's Play* died on a railway line covered with blue paint and so did James Bulger? Baudrillard has no problem with this. It is his 'hyper-reality'. 'The Gulf War,' he proclaims 'didn't really happen.'

2. WOWING THE UNPLUGGED

> To me violence is a totally aesthetic subject.
> Saying you don't like violence in movies is like
> saying you don't like dance sequences in movies.
> Quentin Tarantino.

With David Lynch the horror is mock horror although in no way less realistic. His strange and seedy Gothic romance about the widespread tragedy of malformed children with its echoes of Roman Polanski's *Rosemary's Baby* and Tod Browning's *Freaks*, his crazy waxworks of the final bloodbath scenario in *Blue Velvet*, the boy-hero's 007 Cool as he takes the mobile radio from the frozen standing corpse of the police chief, the realism of Laura's corpse in *Twin Peaks*, show Lynch to be a ragbag, or maybe an elegantly mounted scrapbook, of wide lateral references, all given a cool and seductive irony by the way in which he enhances his fragile skin of bourgeois sanity and order with the visibly cosmetic quality of Norman Rockwell's home scenes. The end of *Blue Velvet* echoes hilariously the tender-hearted gangsters of Cagney and Spencer Tracy. The carnage is impeccable grand guignol. We do not have horror. We have comparable Post-Modernist ideas about different platitudes in the panoply of the horror industry camouflaged in its flawless visual realism, only different from the less explicit horror in, say, Rossellini's *Open City*, in existential terms. The difference lies between the passionate condemnation of political evil in muscular expressionist forms by a man who has initial experience of it, narrative and image springing unselfconsciously and directly from passionate and anguished perceptions, and the sleight-of-hand juggling of the fodder, produced with hi-tec cosmetic camouflage, aimed at the utterly desensitised palates of the citizens of the Rock and Roll Dome. To Rossellini truth is inescapable. Under the Rock and Roll Dome there are many truths, all of them fictions.

So here comes Tarantino in whom the ballet is pure, real guns hammering out real blood in real places, but with such an erudite knowledge of cinema genre that again the response of real caring or real shock, or even of real protest at this freewheeling psychopathy, must be restrained, not to impede the real reception of the movie which is to recognise the tunes and the fast foods mentioned by the characters, to recognise the original movie which is the real origin of each scene, and to revel in the unprecedented obscenity of the dialogue in which Tarantino not only reveals his determination to transpose the scenarios from their original censored era but also to reveal his debt to the astute American street-talk eavesdropping of Elmore Leonard.

Like the leading characters in Lynch's *Wild at Heart*, Tarantino's flip, endearingly inept hit-men are trapped in the perpetual adolescence which Rock and Roll, a culture which denies maturity, imposes. Their schoolyard obscenity whereby every phrase takes on a bad-boy swagger, their erudition in the historic detail of candy bars, soft drinks, burgers, ketchups and top twenty pop songs, shores up a dense protective netting, cutting them off from the grown-up world of ethics, aesthetics, real art, politics and law, even into middle age which ultimately life-style cannot disguise. They are sugared up versions of the label-conscious sadist in Brett Easton Ellis's novel *American Psycho*.

The gathering plethora of screen cruelty (and the comic book cruelty that cross fertilises with it) is, then, like the art which is about art, removed from the initial information of experience in order to address itself to the study, collection and playful reordering of the genres and lexicons of cruelty-depiction that have filtered down over the Rock and Roll years, losing, like conceptual art, any irksome dead weight of outrage, trauma or distress, maintaining, even in such a testing scene as the torture of the cop in *Reservoir Dogs*, a mode of elegance, self-isolating freedom, cool, ostentatious imperviousness to any kind of involvement. The laughter with which the LA audience greeted *Schindler's List* came as no surprise.

Moving on to survey the mode of actual cruelty in the Rock and Roll years it becomes clear that the butchers themselves, whether Fred West or James Bulger's killerinos, have achieved a distancing from the quality of their acts which is exactly parallel to that of the smart cinema audience's distance from their two dimensional holocausts.

3.   PLAYGROUNDS

> I find violence very funny.
>
> Quentin Tarantino.

In the early Sixties two citizens of outer Manchester, low paid office workers in an Oldham run-on-a-shoestring firm, got together an audiotape of Christmas songs and radio Goon Shows. Neddy Seagoon and Bluebottle sounded out between the macabre choral drumbeat of the Little Drummer Boy. Scatty sub-surreal humour alternated with a record anyone might play to their kids to instil the full magic of Christmas as the Christmas fairy actually circles round the tip of the nylon tree in the hall. Brady and Hindley, poor pioneers in their field, were perhaps themselves a little prone to magic still but seemingly a little more prone to the humour of recording the pleas of little Leslie-Ann Downey on the other side of the Christmas tape as they raped her to death.

*

'Make it look witchy,' Charlie said. The hit-persons were a little too scrambled in their synapses to retain such a subtle instruction. They hung up the corpse of the pregnant Sharon Tate, and just like hungry kids always will, made for the fridge and started to scoff supermarket products that Quentin Tarantino would certainly have known the brand names of, one of them sticking a fork in the nearby dome of Sharon Tate's inverted pregnant belly, almost as you might stick it in a baked potato while you chewed, chatted and digested, maybe even enjoyed a spliff between courses.

Charlie had to come back to do the witchy effect himself. He hung the dead along the front garden porch so they could be seen from the boulevard, a scenario which Hollywood would reproduce exactly in fibreglass within the decade.

The Family were photographed while Charlie was awaiting trial. Redolent with sunshine, goodwill and health, they looked like an ad for breakfast cereal. They were embroidering a coat for Charlie so he could wear it during his trial. I don't know whether or not they used a table fork in their weaving techniques.

*

Peter Sutcliffe had a way of situating his victims ready for their discovery. One, for instance, was set in all her sad and graphic splendour, on a wall in one of the little towns around Manchester, all ready for the early rush hour. Another, in a nearby area, was not seen. She was in a hedge surrounding one of those forgotten little fields left behind in the midst of the northern Nineteenth Century industrial spread. Noting no mention of her on the morning radio, much less in the morning papers, Sutcliffe returned to the hedge, hauled the girl out and set her in the middle of the field where the rudimentary spectacle he contrived with her pale, drained limbs could be readily appreciated from the adjacent public ways.

Sutcliffe committed no abominations upon his victims without first killing them, indicating fairly clearly that the extraordinary savagery of his later disfigurements were motivated by his wish to prepare them as a spectacle for whatever unfortunates were to discover them, not in any way by antipathy towards the victim.

148

Two young women in one of the semi-derelict valleys of South Wales had befriended an old woman. Initially they would help her – fetch her tea, her favourite biscuits, a bit of something tasty for supper.

Gradually they made the old woman's flat their second home, their club-room you might say. The old lady became a constant and familiar presence as they took their days and nursed their boredom like a familiar ulcer they were both compelled continually to scratch. Scratching the infection of boredom first involved practical jokes, hiding her knitting, hiding her stick, moving on through greater cruelty (scratch harder, draw blood) like giving her a cup too hot to hold, a cup she (whoops) spills, like tripping her up before she gets to the toilet. Finally she died, burned by cigarettes, battered and fractured. The boredom still itches.

The defendants had to be reprimanded for giggling in the dock, as similar torturers had to be, in similar cases, up and down the nightmare housing estates of the British Isles. There was a need, it seemed, for scarecrow people, people of no further value who could be used as playthings, as pornographic dolls, a general scapegoat punchbag for anybody who'd not quite grown out of the need for something slack, shabby and unresisting to kick.

*

A Manchester group of drug-users had all got rather fed up with Suzanne Capper. Suzanne was a pain in the arse, borrowing things and not giving them back, smoking and sniffing everybody else's stash, whinging and generally being a drag and a bore.

Finally irritation turned to force. They locked her up, first in a room, then in a cupboard, and gave her mind-splintering measures of drugs. In the midst of her consequent temporary paranoic psychosis they hacked off her hair, burnt her, pulled out a couple of her teeth. Word got around that there was a torture scene going on at Number So-and-so, So-and-so Street and people came around, just for a laugh, to see her. Jean, one of the group, tormented her by making a tape. 'Chucky's gonna play,' she said, just like in the movie, *Child's Play*. Then she was taken, naked, in the boot of a car to a nearby park where they poured petrol over her and set light to her.

She extinguished herself and asked two early morning road-menders to help her. They ignored her. Eventually an elderly couple took her in, gingerly wrapped something round her skinless shoulders, and sent for an ambulance.

She was elaborately polite and apologetic to the couple. After being taken to hospital and after naming her torturers to the police, she died.

*

In African states afflicted with internal tribal or political conflict, such as Somalia, Rwanda and Uganda, it has become commonplace for armies of young men to evade the control of their officers and turn the war into a kind of carnival of butchery. In Rwanda this developed into a full-scale spontaneous genocide in which pre-pubescent children were given machetes to get on with the daily task. This was not done with speed and efficiency. Neither was it done with lingering sadism. The executors were often too young to feel much sexual compulsion of that nature. Rather they proceeded with the kind of inventive ludic destructiveness of systematic vandals who must break every small pane in a deserted warehouse.

Women were killed by having their arms and legs cut off, then being thrown into pits to perish. High spirited young men swept through hospitals severing drip-feed and oxygen pipes. Instant informal caesareans were performed without anaesthetic, often with bets having been placed as to the sex of the foetus before the blade swung.

*

America experiences a wave of massacres in its schools carried out by giggling pupils with firearms, some of whom also kill themselves.

*

Three young men drive around Bolton, Lancashire, blithely firing into the crowd.

There is a thread in all this and it is a bright new thread in the ancient fabric of human cruelty. It is the gaiety and the blithe festive joy with which the carnage is carried out. No previous motivation or provocation of cruelty can be brought to account satisfactorily for this new mood of harm. This is not the rigorous work of the political pogrom in which paid executioners are given a grim and tedious daily task of lining people up in mass graves to be shot, of filing people into crematoriums to be gassed and burned. This is no cruelty by ineptitude like the bungled programmes of Nazi concentration camps in the last stages of the Reich. This is not the use of humans as guinea pigs by concentration camp doctors. And sadism is hardly the word. There is no compact here with masochism. It is all too fast and freewheeling to be sex. There is no mesmeric prolonging for intensification of pleasure. Nor is this revenge. Nor the casting off of years of repression. This is definitively aimless and casual.

It is near to, but not quite the same, as the 'two legged hunt' for aborigines much loved by Australian farmers as late as the 1950s. The two legged hunt was, after all, a sport and, as with the sport of the shooting of any game, skill with a firearm was the central concern, not play-sculpture with the human body.

This is more the pulling off of the petals of the human flower, carried out by someone unaware that there is any difference between a human being and a flower. This is the romping of the gleeful mob with knives for people rather than bricks and fire for buildings. The glee is facilitated by a bland failure in the communications system. The access to information which these jolly butchers should have is, at some point, severed. They are without the appraisal of other things that inspire love, wonderment, value, fear, nausea, or identificatory compassion. The reactive wince

150

that swiftly imagines the violence being received, the obvious peril that if it is so easy to dish out, it is easy to receive, is not functioning here.

There even seems to be an equal lack of concern for one's own well-being, for one's own life-rights, for anything. Disregard is the key to the totally arbitrary nature of this swinging of blades and muzzles. The aim seems to be not to shock, nor to terrify but to act out on a large and graphic scale the complete worthlessness of existence. Then the laughter, because finally there has only ever been one joke. It is the breakdown of human control and human purpose – the bishop skids on the banana skin, the Christmas tree blows up, the seagull shits on the lover's eyelid. Laughter is an explosion of relief at the collapse of the notion that we need ever have bothered. Look look! It doesn't matter.

And maybe it's true. Perhaps human beings have finally shaken off the tedious, onerous delusion that they are precious, special and of consequence to one another. Why on earth should human life be sacred? Nothing else is. We raze trees to the ground to pulp them. We eat animals by the megaton. We throw away empty bottles, newspapers, plastic cartons, cars which no longer flatter us, clothes of which we have grown weary. Why should we not become weary of one another and throw one another away?

Is this not the root of the levity? The relief that the bishop has skidded on the banana skin? It's too late to save him and it doesn't matter anyway?

What was it that took the load off our shoulders, that dreadful caring, all that unnecessary guilt, all that love, that pride in workmanship, that boring desire to leave the world a bit better than we found it?

Well, we cast off the notion of desirable domination and submission, especially in the one-to-one love relationship. We rejected that bewildering expansion of the human horizon that Octavio Paz describes in *The Double Flame*, the expansion that occurs when lovers glimpse immortality in one another's souls and find those souls in the exclusive pleasures of one another's bodies. We were not impressed by the fact that the submission between lovers was reciprocal, that lovers made one another exclusive and special to such a degree that they aspired to become one another, and that out of this condition sprang the notion that there was something immortal and special about everyone. Immortality and exclusive importance were a bit like taking a job that required dedication and self-sacrifice. We didn't want vocations. We wanted careers. We wanted to gobble orgasms through a market of human cosmetic accessories designed by the media.

Maybe we hadn't read the Structuralists and the Post-Modernists but we wolfed down the products of people in the media who had. We ditched the idea that culture is somebody's work and somebody's fault. We developed a yawning disdain for those who thought they could change things. We accepted that we were phenomena. Having submitted to such external forces as DNA, electricity and Rock and Roll, the cyber-hive was most acceptable.

In that situation the exact meaning of words, the aesthetic creation of excitement and pleasure, were no longer our concern. We had learned that communication and creation was not what we did. It was a waste of time aspiring to them. Communication was a technology and all we had to do was press the button. Creation had become pretty well a redundant concept. Art was anything done by somebody called an artist and would be made as long as somebody else paid for it.

But best of all, we got rid of the truth, the fact; the silly belief that we are subject to natural conditions in which we don't participate. We learned that we are living a life as it's defined by our culture, that rebellion and subversion are pathetic naiveties. Because DNA chimed with this we had no problem with it, in the way that we had problems with sex as opposed to gender, or beauty as opposed to amusement. All we had to do was wear the clothes and answer to the name. If we wanted to change sex it was a question of gender bending. Wear the clothes, change the name, and if you feel better get somebody to hack you about a bit. Masectomy one way, cut and tuck the other. If you wanted to be a senator, royalty, artist, poet, scientist, war-hero, or maybe waiter, don't attempt the skill or some tedious old paranoid Fascist will tell you you're shite. Just print your business card and announce yourself on the Internet. If truth, like death, gets uncomfortable, tell yourself another truth. If other people are not as you would want them to be, but sick, old, difficult, boring or just plain shabby, avoid them. Stick to the shopping malls and clubs like Stringfellow's where only the privileged and the pretty are admitted.

We don't matter because it's boring to matter, its for the dinosaurs, the digitariat. If we've achieved one thing in our era it's to unload the awful weight of the illusion of human significance.

Lyall Watson, the Darwinian anthropologist, went to Liverpool to see with his own eye Jon Venables and Robert Thompson, James Bulger's killers. He describes one of them thus: 'As Robert Thompson left his seat he looked briefly at the public seats behind him, and it wasn't boredom or indifference that he showed. Those are emotions, negative ones to be sure but nevertheless emotional states that are suggestive of response. There was nothing in Robert Thompson's eyes. Nothing whatsoever. None of the glare that police officers had found difficult to explain. It was a blank face and yet not one frozen still in shock: just blank, a mask without identity, dead skin over dead eyes.'

Well *of course* there was nothing there. This is our discovery. There never was anything there. We can do anything or we can do nothing. There is no reason one way or the other. This is what we have found out.

A short time ago Kilroy-Silk, the low-viewing-time Oprah from Brum, ran a show on bullying. Present in the studio were some victims, their parents, some parents of children who had killed themselves through bullying, and some bullies. Main spokesmen among the bullies were two quite exquisite teenage girls, one black, one a white blonde. They had spent a lot of time and money on making sure they were

152

exquisite. The black girl had her hair in little sculptured waves that clung to her forehead reminiscent of Josephine Baker. The lips of the blonde were perfectly painted with a very subtle, barely perceptible outline. The dictates of fashion were perfectly observed. The care with which they had both toed the line demanded by their culture was impressive. Together they had driven their victim to attempt suicide and when she failed to do so had sent her pills with the instructions to try again. Both smiled as they recounted this. Neither showed any regrets.

The victims were an interesting contrast. They were just kids, prone to hesitation in speech, unremarkable in their looks, weepy and reliant on the parents who accompanied them. The bullies were alone. They relied on no-one and seemed to believe that their smartness had in some way rendered them inviolable.

It became clear that a self-presentation so valued, a smartness that had replaced the securities of family love, indeed of any love, would be threatened by the proximity of ordinary, semi-shambolic, human, idiosyncratic kids. The bullying was surely self-protective. 'Get out of my penumbra, mortal!'

The pair precipitated a tirade led by a formidable middle-aged Scotswoman whose tongue lashed them for a good two or three minutes. Then the fury of a whole studio full of people poured around their ears. And then, very gradually, they became slightly crestfallen. Their pertness and their poise wilted. They were not yet ashamed. That was far too much to hope for. But they were scared. They had realised that it was maybe going to be a problem getting home without being attacked. They had glimpsed reality. They were experiencing what I've called initial information throughout this text.

For the luxurious irresponsibility we have achieved by the systematic dismantling of certainties is an error and the corrective to this error is experience, the appraisal of something with our undeceived, uncontorted and unconditioned instincts and senses, and the highly skilled, cutting edge of this appraisal is art.

The play with substitute bodies by Jake and Dinos Chapman and the play with animal bodies by Damien Hirst has the same disregard for the function and the sacredness of the body as that evidenced by Robert Thompson. The qualities of real shock and outrage have been disconnected. However dreadful the event, infantile silliness is all the artists can bring to it.

If convinced perceptions, so strong that they detonate vomiting, weeping, orgasm or love are defused by relativist philosophy, by uncaring ignorance licensed as street wisdom, and by deluding drugs which, after continual use, cast all experience under a self-protective scepticism towards what may be only an hallucination, then, indeed, the individual cruising aimlessly in a penumbral vacuum of personal space, may, and indeed will, do anything at all, especially indulge in cruel play, to perpetually test the freedom of his isolation, his severance from other things, and to test his release from any of the historic panoply of progress, creativity, justice and kindness that is contingent on the acknowledgement of other things in any certain definition. A valued imperviousness to experience must be tested and wanton, unrestrained cruelty is a fine way to do it.

In such a condition casual self-pleasuring is the only mandate and the only goal whether by masturbation or by monetary gain. In the interests of this much simplified human goal we must cut out our hearts. Otherwise we might lose our cool and actually start to realise with some dismay that everything we've ever built over 6000 years is disintegrating, leaving society in ruins.

INDEX

(illustrations appear in italics)